BITE-SIZED MARKETING

realistic solutions for the overworked librarian

Nancy Dowd, Mary Evangeliste, & Jonathan Silberman

American Library Association

Chicago   2010

The paper used in this publication meets the minimum requirements of American National Standard for Information Sciences—Permanence of Paper for Printed Library Materials, ANSI Z39.48-1992. ∞

Library of Congress Cataloging-in-Publication Data

Dowd, Nancy, 1956–

  Bite-sized marketing : realistic solutions for the overworked librarian / Nancy Dowd, Mary Evangeliste, and Jonathan Silberman.

    p.   cm.

  ISBN 978-0-8389-1000-9 (alk. paper)

  1. Libraries—Marketing. 2. Libraries—Public relations. I. Evangeliste, Mary. II. Silberman, Jonathan, 1982– III. Title.

Z716.3.D69 2010

021.7—dc22   2009016829

ISBN-13: 978-0-8389-1000-9

Printed in the United States of America
14 13 12 11 10   5 4 3 2 1

Nancy Dowd

is director of marketing for the New Jersey State Library, where she incorporates her career experiences as an editor, writer, presenter, and marketer to produce effective and replicable marketing strategies for libraries. Her marketing campaign featuring the Easy Readers calendar transformed the image of librarians and received international attention. Her work has received awards from the American Library Association, the New Jersey Library Association, Public Relations Society of America NJ, and *Information Today*. She is the author of two blogs, *The M Word* and *The Best of Library Videos*.

Mary Evangeliste

has more than fifteen years of experience in the fine arts and in libraries. She has taught, lectured, and presented in the areas of art history, librarianship, and marketing for local and national groups including the State Department, the Maryland School of Art and Design, Prince George's Community College, the University of Pittsburgh, the Library Administration and Management Association, the Association of College and Research Libraries, and the ALA. She is the cofounder of Fearless Future and the director of User Services and Outreach at Musselman Library, Gettsburg College. She holds a BA in art history from Allegheny College and an MLIS in library and information science from the University of Pittsburgh. Mary has been honored with two national library marketing awards, 3M Check-It-Out Yourself Day and ACRL's 2005 Best Practices in Marketing Academic and Research Libraries @ your library Award.

Jonathan Silberman

is an award-winning graphic designer who helps nonprofits and educational institutions develop marketing and identity systems. Before cofounding his design and marketing consulting firm, Fearless Future, with his business partner, Mary Evangeliste, he worked as a freelance designer for more than ten years. His first experience as the designer for the marketing team at American University Library was honored by ACRL with the 2005 Best Practices in Marketing Academic and Research Libraries @ your library Award. Jonathan's designs have been used in international and national library presentations on marketing, such as the International Federation of Library Associations and Institutions, ACRL, LAMA, and ALA.

Contents

We've all been sold a bill of goods that whenever you attempt marketing, it has to be *grand*. It has to be a logo redesign or a complete overhaul of your building.

This book puts that assumption to rest. It is about integrating marketing into every day and making it manageable.

Introduction

When we began this book we thought we would be able to produce ten-minute marketing solutions for librarians, but the truth is that nothing worthwhile can get done in ten minutes. Instead, we have created a book with tangible ideas that can be done in bite-sized chunks. You can flip open this book whenever you need to choose a strategy. Don't let the idea of marketing become overwhelming; pick a strategy and try it out on a product, inject some excitement into your organization, and then figure out what works.

Marketing goes beyond trying to get people to use your library; it is a concerted effort to articulate your value. It is that plain and simple.

The shortcuts we offer you are about simplifying and streamlining your processes. All good marketing always takes into account a customer's need and includes an evaluation. In between is the magic that we will share with you.

The real secret to marketing? *Just try.*

Word-of-Mouth Marketing

1

A New Paradigm Has Emerged

Libraries have finally gotten a break in the marketing arena. In the old days advertising agencies charged companies small fortunes to create campaigns for them and then spent another fortune to push the message out to the consumer through television, radio, and print ads. While those companies paid a million dollars for Super Bowl commercials, libraries barely could get public service announcements played on local radio stations. Even if libraries had wanted to get in the game, few would have had enough money to launch a campaign. Then came the Internet and with it the emergence of a new wave of consumer-driven marketing. Communication networks have evolved into social networks, Web 2.0 technology has provided tools that replace the need for million-dollar budgets, and the new style of word-of-mouth marketing has emerged. The stars have aligned: this new era of marketing makes it possible for any library to reach any audience with a message about its programs, products, and services. This portal of equality will not last forever; corporations are putting all their energies into getting ahead of the pack, and we need to act now. The caveat is that we will not drive this new era; our customers will. Our mission, if we chose to accept it, is to reach out to our customers to help us promote libraries to existing and potential customers and to develop advocacy networks to ensure future funding. We can start by understanding and adopting the strategies of word-of-mouth marketing.

Libraries had smart and new ideas. Wherever we went we told people about those ideas. We found ways to share our ideas through newsletters, posters, blogs, YouTube videos, Internet forums, and e-mail. That didn't really work for libraries, though, because the key ingredient—getting others to spread the word for us—was missing. The time for excuses is over. If libraries could have invented a specific marketing technique that would work best for us, it would have been word-of-mouth marketing.

What Is Word-of-Mouth Marketing?

Word-of-mouth marketing (WOMM) centers on the concept that 10 percent of the population influences the behavior of the other 90 percent. To create a successful WOMM campaign, we just have to get those influencers on board, give them the proper information, and provide the tools to help them share that information. Then they'll spread our message to everyone else, and that message will have more impact than anyone could imagine.

Word-of-mouth marketing has always been a powerful influencer and is fast becoming the driving force behind today's marketing. Thanks to the Internet, people now have tools to help them share their thoughts not only with friends and relatives but also with people all over the world. Those same tools provide a creative outlet for influencers to create their own messages, which results in campaigns filled with an array of videos, blog posts, podcasts, and other personal commentaries that surpass any results you may have imagined.

The question for libraries is not whether we will harness the power of WOMM but how and to what degree.

Libraries have earned customer loyalty by listening to the needs of our customers, who often express their satisfaction or praise either verbally or in writing. What we have not capitalized on is the new WOMM techniques in which campaigns are specifically designed to help those satisfied customers share that praise with their friends, family, neighbors, and fellow workers instead of telling us. Word-of-mouth marketing is not about libraries gathering testimonies and telling the community how great we are doing. It is about helping our customers create the buzz. By using WOMM techniques, libraries can leverage the power and pervasiveness of word of mouth and put it to work for their programs, products, and services in a replicable and measurable way.

What Makes WOMM So Powerful?

People trust the recommendations from people they know over those of a stranger. What is amazing about WOMM is that online relationships

> The trick to a successful WOMM campaign is to make sure that you reach and give tools to spread the word to the 10 percent of people who will influence the other 90 percent.

What Is WOMM?

It's all about the product.

How many times has your library offered a program, product, or service that excited the staff but never caught on with the public?

We are quick to say that libraries need to advertise, educate, and inform the public about our services. However, the real problem may be that the library as a product doesn't fill a need for our public.

The first step in any WOMM campaign is to make sure you have a product that stirs passion in the hearts of your customers and that allows you to have two-way conversations with them.

> If you don't have a service that will generate passion among a group of people, you must stop what you're doing and start over.
>
> —Seth Godin

are forming with a virtual connection, sometimes between people who have never met each other face-to-face.

For many librarians, the idea that people would choose to listen to a nonauthoritative source goes against the fundamental belief that people need experts as guides. Those librarians might hesitate to use the full power of personal recommendations. This brings to mind the arguments that some librarians had voiced against Google and Wikipedia. They were always good arguments, but when push came to shove, the public drove the outcome, not the well-thought-out arguments of librarians. Like it or not, we are in a populist age, and the days of people wanting to hear from authoritative sources are passing by very quickly. If we want to deliver a message, we need to know what people want, develop the product that fills that need, and then give people the tools to spread the word for us. That is WOMM.

Philosophy of WOMM

Consumers are an interesting lot. We pride ourselves on our judgment to choose the best. Whether we just got the best price or best product at the best location, the idea is that we made a good choice. When we make good choices, we are proud to share them with our friends because it reflects our good judgment. Word-of-mouth marketing makes it easier for people to share their stories.

Consumers are passionate about companies for many reasons. They might like the product or simply believe that the company warrants support because it reflects their values. Although it is always good to have people like your product, having someone identify with your organization because he or she identifies it with personal values is also very powerful. Businesses know this and are always trying to make the connection between their companies and popular causes or to create branding that appeals to consumers' inner consciousness. The beauty of libraries is that our intrinsic values apply to everyone from traditionalists who believe that libraries are fundamental to healthy communities to trendsetters who believe that libraries are community centers transforming lives. The key for libraries is to connect the dots for people and be willing to rebrand those core values to help our customers identify with them. The way to get people in our doors is not to convince them that we have the materials they need but to help them feel that by using our materials they are becoming the kind of person they want to be.

Keeping up with the latest trends will help your library remain relevant to your customers. Finding new trends can be incredibly easy. Just by living in the world, talking with your friends and family, and being connected you can start on the path to being a trend watcher. For example, personal learning environments are a current trend. Libraries have always provided lifelong learning opportunities, but now we might want to promote the idea that we offer personal learning environments.

> **Libraries are perfectly positioned to be major players in the current economic crisis. People need hope, inspiration, training, and opportunities. Sounds like a good slogan, doesn't it?**

The reasoning behind WOMM began as a simple concept. Produce a product that people can be passionate about, get it into the hands of those people whose opinion other people respect, give the influencers the tools to share their satisfaction, and let them influence people they know and drive people to use your product. It sounds so simple that it makes you wonder why we don't use WOMM for all our products. Well, the thing about WOMM is that it requires organizations to change up a few things in order to be effective.

Mainly, that means that customers have to love what you offer enough to want to talk about it.

A Bad Rap for Libraries

Before we go any further, this seems a good time to talk about the bad rap libraries have with people who don't use libraries. There are lots of people who won't go near a library and others who may take their children but never consider using the library for their own needs. We just met a librarian the other day who said that her friends and family think she's nuts for wanting a job that will keep her in a library all day. Even Nancy's hairdresser sounded proud of the fact that he hadn't been to a library since college. For those of us who love libraries, it's really difficult to imagine this kind of thinking. But it exists, and if you are going to transcend the bad rap, you're going to need to tackle this head-on. That means bringing those negative opinions into the light, getting some input from people to help you change things, and energizing some influencers to spread the word about the changes. This doesn't have to be a huge librarywide process. You can narrow down your target audience and enact changes that will affect them without changing your whole library. Then if you are successful, you can consider expanding the program.

Start by Turning On a Flashlight

Libraries love focus groups but not always the straight talk that we need to hear. Why not start with a simple survey to shine a light on the real reasons people aren't using your library and to recruit a few influencers at the same time? Take a quick survey out to a local bookstore, a grocery store that offers video rentals, a theater, or a night school and ask a few nonusers a few questions about why they don't use the library. Pick places that offer products that match what your library provides to ensure that you are surveying true potential customers. Follow up by asking for advice in making changes. It is amazing to have the input of dedicated nonusers to create change and then have them turn on their friends to the library!

Approach people with this question:

We're surveying people who don't use the library. Do you qualify?

Want to really reach the nonusers? Try this question:

We're looking for people who wouldn't be caught dead in a library. Do you qualify?

Example Questionnaire

1. Why don't you use your local library? (Check all answers that apply.)

☐ I'd rather buy my books.

☐ I hate fines.

☐ I hate books.

☐ I don't like the way librarians talk to me.

☐ I have to wait too long to get a book.

☐ I don't like the smell of borrowed books.

☐ It reminds me of school too much.

☐ I have no idea where to find what I want.

☐ The librarians are too intimidating.

☐ It doesn't mesh with my lifestyle.

☐ It's not convenient.

☐ It's not cool.

☐ It's for children.

☐ The programs are boring.

☐ No one I know uses it.

☐ I owed a fine and never went back.

☐ It's too far away.

☐ The building is too small.

☐ It doesn't have enough computers.

☐ I don't like to read.

☐ It doesn't have the kind of books I read, such as _____
_____

☐ I don't watch DVDs.

☐ I only listen to music that I download.

☐ Other _____

2. Do you personally know anyone who uses the library?

3. If yes, who? (*This question will give you an idea of how close the respondent's social network is to the library. The farther away the network is from the library, the better your chances are of bringing in an entire new population to your library if the respondent becomes an advocate of the library!*)

☐ Personal friend

☐ Fellow worker

☐ Classmate

☐ Parent

☐ Sibling

☐ Child

☐ Neighbor

☐ Online friend

....

When you get the survey back, ask whether there is anything a library could do or offer that would bring the person in. Write those answers down. Ask whether he or she would be willing to look over the plan if the library decided to follow up on the suggestion. If you get a yes, you'll have your first influencer.

This survey may shed a harsh light on how nonusers view your library. It may not. In any case, you will have a much better idea of the obstacles you will have to overcome in creating and marketing new programs.

Whenever I did surveys I found the best way to get a good response and good variety was to go where the people are. We often sat in the social services offices, medical clinics, etc. It was amazing the response—often you could get quite a conversation going and not only get your surveys completed, but do some excellent promoting of your library.

—Pam Jaskot, *library consultant for communications, State Library of North Carolina*

Basic Elements of WOMM

1. Identify the influencers.
2. Create simple ideas that are easy to communicate.
3. Give people the tools they need to spread the word.
4. Host a conversation.
5. Evaluate and measure.

The Influencers

The people who convey your message can have a major impact on whether others accept that message. For large-scale campaigns you'll want to find the 10 percent who can influence the other 90 percent of your population. Influencers have been called sneezers, buzz agents, fans, advocates, friends, or even cool kids. No matter what you choose to label them, finding people who are excited about what you are doing and who want to tell others is the most essential ingredient in any WOMM campaign.

One of our staff members is paid but also a member of our Friends. Bless her heart—she is over seventy-five years old but she is a human dynamo. She also belongs to the Golden Seniors in our town—a fairly active group of 250 or so (our town's population is approximately nine thousand). She manages to finagle all of these groups and individual library users into buying tickets, attending events, buying books from the book sale, donating to the library or just dropping in to read the paper! She is a living marvel—I only wish I had her energy and tenacity! But she is a great one for spreading the word—she often knows town news before anyone else and so she loves to tell it too—which is great for us!

—Jane Kingsland, *Township of Washington Public Library*

How to Identify Influencers

Influencers are easy to identify. Look for people with a charismatic personality and persuasive communication style and with a social network. Having influencers spread your message will dramatically increase your ability to get buy-in for your campaign.

Some influencers reach huge amounts of people; others reach a small niche group. The key characteristic of influencers is that people want to listen to them. They are leaders of social groups, influential bloggers, community

Here are some sample posts to attract influencers:

Free iTunes

Check out our brand-new program, share your honest opinion with people you know, and provide us with input and feedback to help us make this the kind of program teens really want. You'll get a free iTunes download just for signing up and the chance to win an iPod.

Register here [connect to a simple e-mail registration form]

For further information call: Libby 555-1212 or e-mail: libby@anylibrary.com

Have a Say in the Kinds of Programs Your Library Hosts!

We are looking to improve our schedule of live performances. Whether authors, musicians, poets, politicians, athletes, or business leaders, we believe in the powerful interaction that happens during a live performance. We are looking for people to share their honest opinions with individuals they know and to provide us with input and feedback to help us offer the kind of performances our community members really want.

Register here [connect to a simple e-mail registration form]

For further information call: Libby 555-1212 or e-mail: libby@anylibrary.com

You can never get enough influencers. Create an entire list of all different areas in which you are looking for input, post them on the same web page, and let people choose the ones that appeal to their interests.

leaders, and reporters. Don't forget the social networks. Look for online groups such as Facebook, MySpace, and message boards.

Needless to say, you don't want to ignore the other 90 percent of the population. In fact, if you can get your message out to your target audience and it resonates with enough people and those people each influence two friends, you can have pretty powerful results.

Tips for Recruiting Influencers

There are several ways to recruit influencers. Probably the easiest way is to ask people to participate through a post on related web pages, blogs, posters, fliers, newsletters, and any other promotional materials you create that are geared for the target audience.

Better yet, ask your customers directly. Be clear, write your material to your specific target audience, and let them know what you need and what they'll get out of it.

Provide Incentives

What will people get in return for playing along with you? Surprising enough, incentives don't always have to be material rewards. Social status is a huge motivator as well. When Facebook developed its Causes application, it rewarded influencers by listing the top achievers in a hall of fame. Even if you do offer material incentives, they can be as small as a ninety-nine-cent iTunes download. One librarian for teens swears by lollipops. If you're not sure what kind of incentives will work, then ask. Just be sure to follow through on the suggestions.

Now that we're talking about incentives, here are the reasons one of the oldest WOMM and media network companies, BzzAgent (at www.bzzagent .com), gives its recruits:

Top 5 Reasons to join the BzzAgent network:

1. Discover and experience new products and services first
2. Prove that your voice and opinions matter
3. Always have something to talk about with friends
4. Be part of a growing international network of more than 400,000 consumers
5. Find pirate treasure—or influence companies and brands

Have fun creating your incentive lists. Appeal to the internal incentives of your customers, especially microcommunities. Look at the mission statements from the hobby groups, business organizations, or community groups and play with that wording.

Make Your Customers Special

The secret weapon to WOMM is to allow your customers to be on the inside of the campaign. Let them play a role in the creation process and provide opportunities for them to create new content like commercials, logos, and the like. Give your influencers a VIP pass for first access to information and content. People who are involved in the process make enthusiastic influencers.

Follow Up with Results

Let your influencers know how the project is going and how they have positively affected the campaign. If the campaign is having problems, ask them for input. If you decide to discontinue a project, offer influencers the opportunity to continue on other projects.

Create Simple, Easy-to-Communicate Messages

What do you want your influencers to tell their friends? The message has to be simple. Remember the game telephone? One person begins by whispering a sentence to the person next to him or her and that person whispers the sentence to the next person until it gets to the last person. When the last person announces the sentence it is usually something entirely different. Well, WOMM is a lot like that game. So keep your message simple!

Things to keep in mind when you develop a message:

+ Keep it simple.
+ Make it memorable.
+ Turn it into a story.
+ Include a call to action.

Give Influencers Cool Tools

Remember, WOMM doesn't begin until someone spreads your message. Up until that moment, you have created just a traditional marketing campaign. Not all of your influencers will promote your organization through face-to-face contact. It is crucial to provide different ways for people to share your message. Be sure to create different key messages for the different ways people will share your message.

For example, some people like to clip newspaper articles to share with friends, but others like to e-mail articles to a friend. To have both types of people share an article from your newsletter, you need to offer people the opportunity to either print the article or e-mail it from your web page. There may be another population who doesn't read news on the Web at all—they will need copies printed out for them.

If cost is a factor for printing materials such as newsletters, set up a print-on-demand center at your library. Use an old computer and upload PDFs of all your brochures and news articles to the desktop. For newsletters, list individual articles rather than the entire newsletter. Let people print what they need for free. You can keep track of what people print out as a way to measure success.

Your job is to give influencers the tools to promote you wherever they are. So for the face-to-face (F2F) folks, handouts and bookmarks will probably work. But once they are online, they'll need gadgets and applications for their desktops, mobile phones, and web spaces; RSS feeds; and links to your web pages. These widgets are continually evolving. It may not be too long down the road that they'll pop up in cars and even refrigerators. (Imagine being able to give a widget to your customers that would post new programs through the computer in their refrigerators!) Don't get discouraged if you aren't up to date on the latest widgets, because your influencers will be. They'll not only let you know which ones work best but can probably create them for you. Just ask!

Create a Toolbox to Help Spread Your Messages

In the old days libraries provided bookmarks and fliers for people to share with their friends and family. Now we have an incredible array of tools, and new ones are being developed every day. There are some pretty standard tools that every library should have in place for WOMM efforts. You don't have to be cutting edge, but as certain tools gain popularity it only makes sense to include them as part of your toolbox.

A very basic toolbox would include the following:

- Printed materials, such as bookmarks, rack cards, or brochures, that people can hand out to friends
- Website, wiki, and/or blog where you can provide information and stories and host conversations with your customers
- A social networking page such as MySpace or Facebook
- Video posted to an online service such as YouTube
- Pictures posted to Flickr and/or social networking pages
- Microblog, like Twitter or Pownce
- Widgets to allow people to share on their favorites sites, such as SocialTwist and ShareThis (if you see a button on a web page, click through; if the code is free, you can use it as a tool on your own site)

Take a look at the fantastic article at the website Digital Inspiration, "How to Post Anything to the Web," by Amit Agarwal. We heard about it from the Central Jersey Regional Library Cooperative technology blog at http://cjrlctech.blogspot.com.

Host a Conversation

Your organization must be willing to host open conversations about your library that include your customers' needs and opinions. This is a biggie because those conversations may not always be positive, which may be difficult for some libraries to allow. But without an open exchange you'll never be able to harness the full power of customer influencers to spread the word. Once your library accepts the idea of a customer-driven product, you can create a structure that will nurture WOMM.

You can host online conversations in places such as blogs, wikis, message boards, and social networks. Offline conversations can take place too. A whiteboard with markers is a great place to encourage conversations.

Connecting Online and Offline Conversations

As great as online social networks are, there is a growing recognition of a need for people who hook up online to connect in person. The F2F interaction isn't replacing online social networks, but it is strengthening the quality of those conversations and interactions. Companies are catching on that they can get on board by positioning their company in the center of the F2F meet up.

For example, you could take an online network like Facebook, add the library as an offline place to meet, and then stir in something really cool like an author visit to give people a reason to get together. Yahoo!'s Jason Anello spoke about this trend at the 2008 WOMM Summit. An example he used was the airline KLM's Club Africa. The airline created exclusive clubs for frequent fliers who conduct business in certain areas of the world. Members of the select group are given opportunities to network both online and offline, and they have access to exclusive events and services.

Anello suggested three things that companies can do to take advantage of this trend:

- Figure out where your company is most relevant in the real-world environment.
- Look for existing links between this space and the spaces where your customers hang out online.
- Create an experiment that connects people simultaneously in both spaces.

This is a great concept for libraries because we are in a perfect position to create destinations locally and all over the world.

Building Trust with Your Administration

The great thing about Web 2.0 is that we now have the tools to reach our audiences directly. The trouble is that those tools create a very open process, and that type of public discussion can be a double-edged sword for public institutions. You need to find a balance between being open and protecting your institution. You have your judgment, and you want be as open as possible, but if it goes off the rails you have to be willing to pull back. It is easier to open up the process than to close it back down, so start small and keep communicating with your administrators throughout the process.

Transparency Won't Guarantee They'll Come, but It's Almost a Sure Bet They Won't Come without It

There is nothing new about friends sharing their opinions with friends. What is new is how they are doing it. With the Internet people can be heard around the world. They are invited to post their stories on CNN, to write book reviews on Amazon.com, and to create music lists on iTunes. It is the age of public discourse and the everyman expert. While Amazon reviews and LibraryThing have found successful formulas for interacting with their customers, many libraries are still struggling to allow people to post comments on their blogs.

The problem with not moving ahead is that we are missing the shift in the way people communicate. People like reading what other people write because it sparks ideas about what they think and encourages them to write something themselves. When we were kids and got in trouble for following a friend, our parents would ask, "If Bobby jumped off a bridge, would you follow him?" Back then the question was rhetorical. Today the answer would be, "You betcha!"

Not only do we need to host the conversation, but we need to engage in it as well. Transparency is all about organizations listening, responding, and sharing the process. It's about letting strangers have an impact on how things are done.

Here are three simple ways libraries can be more transparent:

- Allow moderated comments on blogs.
- Publicly respond to complaints. Let people know what you will do to resolve the problem.
- Allow people to write reviews about books, movies, programs, and so on, and link from your site or allow them space on yours.

12 Signposts for the Transparent Library, from Michael Casey and Michael Stephens

1. Give everyone an avenue to talk.

2. Play nice and be constructive.

3. Grow and develop your support community.

4. Be willing to accept anonymity.

5. Tell the truth.

6. Focus on user-driven policy, not driving users away.

7. Have an open-door policy.

8. Participate in the conversation.

9. Measure progress.

10. Serve all of your user groups.

11. Check your ego at the door.

12. Embrace change.

Source: "The Transparent Library: Six Signposts," www.libraryjournal.com/article/CA6611609 .html?rssid=220; "The Transparent Library: Six More Signposts," www.libraryjournal.com/ article/CA6618868.html?q=transparent.

Be careful that you don't get caught in the trap of positive testimony and call it WOMM. Positive testimonies are usually solicited and reflect a positive aspect of your organization. The testimonies are great and serve a purpose in marketing your library. However, even when they have a truly compelling character or story, they won't inspire others to speak up. Authentic reviews come from people's hearts. They will most likely be negative or at least mention a complaint. They have imperfections like words spelled wrong, bad sound tracks, or shaky camera work, but the core message strikes a chord in the person who is reading, listening, or watching that makes that person identify so strongly that he or she wants to speak up too. And that is where WOMM is born.

Evaluate and Reevaluate

Evaluation is a little different in WOMM because we need to measure the things that are relevant to our success. Traditional numbers don't always work for WOMM campaigns. You might get a million hits on a YouTube video, but not one of them is from the United States, much less your community. Or your message could go viral after the event has taken place—which is not much help if you had counted on people attending the fund-raiser.

One of the new measurement trends that could work for libraries is to measure customer engagement and track how your customers progress from tool to tool on their path to the outcome they desire.

The Word of Mouth Marketing Association has begun to create a new measurement system. It divides each occurrence that can occur into a WOMM communication and creates two categories: object and quality. It then evaluates the who, how, what, and where accordingly. It sounds a little complicated, but the association has published a report on its website and will be updating it as it learns more. What is important for libraries is to begin looking at measuring results as a process rather than as a concrete number.

The New-Media Marketing Manifesto

I will address the needs of the new customer.

I will recognize that my customers are the experts; they are authors, graphic designers, directors, and virtual explorers.

I will respect that my customers are passionate and want to be in control.

I will always ask my customers what they need and will work to give it to them.

I will work to provide my customers places to meet in person, on the phone, online, or even in the virtual world.

I will work to ensure that my customers have tools that allow them to communicate wherever they are and that are personalized to their specific desires.

I will remember that my job is not to convince people that they need libraries but to convince libraries that they need people.

I will no longer use outdated marketing techniques of pushing out messages and hoping to get a bite.

I will use new marketing by giving over the microphone to the customers and letting them communicate the message.

I will recognize the need for an open dialogue with my customers.

WOMM Checklist

☐ **Find and Encourage Influencers**

+ Search online at blogs and social networks to find people who are talking about your library and leave a comment thanking them for mentioning your library. If they criticize the library, tell them that you are interested in helping and begin a conversation toward a solution.

+ Search for people or groups that would be interested in topics relevant to your product and invite them to be a special participant, to offer input, or to just sign up to receive news.

+ Keep up to date with communications.

+ Give them public recognition or an elevated status. Praise them on your blog, include their names in your newsletters, or just create spotlights on your sites. Let others know they are valued.

☐ **Is Your Message Simple?**

+ Have you made it memorable?

+ Have you created a story that others can tell?

+ Did you include a call to action to let them know what you need them to do, like "Visit our website," or "Sign up for the program"?

☐ **Cool Tools**

+ Is everything easy to share with others?

+ Remove all barriers that would keep people from downloading, remixing, and sharing your materials by providing permission such as Creative Commons licenses.

+ Provide a Microsoft Word version of any online PDF files so people can cut and paste to their blogs.

+ Move content from your web page to places where it is easier for people to find and share, such as blogs, Flickr, YouTube, SlideShare, and the like.

+ Add a Tell a Friend link on every web page.

Hosting a Conversation

+ Have you provided online and offline places for customers to gather, communicate, and have fun?

+ Have you maintained transparency?

+ Are you encouraging authentic conversations between you and your customers?

+ Have you created ongoing and clear communication with your administrators?

Evaluate

+ Are you measuring the elements that are relevant to your efforts?

+ Are you using built-in analytics for blogs?

+ Have you considered installing Google Analytics?

A note about library book reviews and WOMM: Many libraries have created opportunities for children to write book reviews that are posted online. While there is merit in having kids write book reviews that resemble book reports, the reviews people contribute online are authentic opinions written because the person felt compelled to say something about the book. It is essential to understand that there is a difference between a child writing a review for a library as part of an assignment from a teacher or librarian and a person writing a review because he or she wants to say something. The latter is the basis of WOMM and has the possibility of attracting others to participate.

Libraries and the Long Tail

When Chris Anderson spoke at the ALA Annual Conference in New Orleans several years ago, he made the point that libraries are in a perfect position to take advantage of the long tail. Think about it. Libraries have the ability to create products for all those small passionate groups within a community. And the Internet and mobile devices allow us to easily tap into social networks to connect with those audiences without spending a fortune.

Have you figured out what trends your influencers are talking about and made the connection to your library? Host an online discussion or a live event. Ask them for their ideas and act on it.

Types of WOMM That Work Well for Libraries

Buzz Marketing

Buzz marketing is where WOMM all began. The formula begins with an exciting news event or a high-profile celebrity endorsement that gets people talking, or buzzing, about your organization. While we often think that these types of campaigns have to be launched in large national or state venues, creating a buzz for any niche market works, and in the nonprofit arena, smaller is definitely better.

Caution! Unless it's tagged with a viral component that gets others to carry the buzz, everything can fizzle into a onetime phenomenon and quickly become yesterday's news.

What Is "Going Viral"?

Just as a virus can infect an entire community, viral marketing uses messages designed to pass from person to person and gain momentum as they go along. "Going viral" means that a campaign has caught momentum and has taken on a life of its own. All WOMM campaigns are designed to go viral to one degree or another. Viral campaigns that go worldwide are neat, but for a local campaign, good local buzz will do the job for you.

Niche Marketing

Back in 2004, the editor of *Wired* magazine, Chris Anderson, wrote about long-tail marketing, or how the big online companies were having success by selling their products to a large number of small niche markets. The basic idea is that while the larger companies will capture 20 percent of the market, the other 80 percent of the market consists of smaller niche markets. With the advent of the Internet, it is now possible to reach those small markets throughout the world. Companies like Amazon.com have tapped into the long tail by selling a few books to a wide range of those niche markets.

Community Marketing

Communities that share the same interests can communicate your message among themselves. You provide the tools, content, and information to assist them. This should really be called library marketing, because it is a perfect way to develop and support the special collections in our libraries.

Influencer Marketing

Influencer marketing identifies key communities and opinion leaders who are likely to talk about your organization and have the ability to influence the opinions of others. Cultivating influencers to take a leadership role in spreading your message can have a powerful impact. We need to wrap bright yellow caution tape around this one because there is a thin line between an inspiring influencer and an overzealous person who fluctuates between boring and annoying.

Grassroots Marketing

Calling on volunteers to engage in local outreach for your organization requires you to organize and provide the motivation that will start a movement. This can be very effective for nonprofits. The only drawback is that you will inevitably lose control over how others conduct their outreach. The idea of not having control over message delivery is a recurring theme in WOMM, but when it comes to grassroots efforts, concentrate on the passion of the outreach and overlook details that aren't done the way your organization would prefer. You can keep your brand and messaging intact by creating outreach kits. Depending on the budget, the kit can be comprehensive with promotional materials and tabletop displays or as simple as a handout with major talking points for your activists.

WOMM with Social Networks

Facebook, MySpace, Virb, Pownce, or any of the countless other networking sites can be great places for people to spread good messages about your organization.

One drawback of marketing with any of the social networks is the continual censorship by certain organizations such as schools that may prevent access for students and teachers. Be on the lookout for other places where censorship may take place. Some companies are taking measures to prevent employees from accessing certain sites in an effort to increase productivity.

The thing about social networks is that they were developed to be both social and personal. Effective WOMM taps into the power of social networking by letting network members talk about you. It is essential to be authentic, and that means finding people in the network who want to pass on your message. It will not work for you to pretend—today's consumer has an instinctive sense for almost instantly spotting a poser. Keep it real or don't do it.

New ideas are always being developed. Facebook is continually evolving to create tools that can help nonprofits create authentic connections with supporters. You can create a Facebook page for your library to serve as an online information center. At the page, people can sign up to be your "fan," in Facebook lingo, so they can get information that you post directly to their profile pages. The great thing about these pages is that you get to see your fans and can tailor the message to your audience. Another way you can use Facebook is to bring together passionate users by creating a group and letting them have a voice in what they want or need from the library.

Ideas to Tie Together Social Networks and the Offline Community

+ Talk with staff members who have their own profiles on a social network. Encourage them to be influencers by making suggestions about programs, products, or services that might be of interest to their online friends and by setting up online interest polls on their pages.

+ Publicize your new group in the library and mention it at all of your events or computer classes.

+ Give a class on social networks and invite everyone to join your group.

+ Invite social network groups to select a book each month for your library to purchase, with the agreement that if you purchase it, they will market it to the people they know. Invite them to host a meet up in your library.

Web 2.0 Tools at Work

If there is any doubt about the power of Web 2.0 tools, then just take a look at Barack Obama's presidential campaign. It was classic WOMM. What is even more exciting is that he is already continuing to use the format to communicate directly with the American public. If you look at the elements of his campaign, you'll see the making of a best practice for WOMM. Something to keep in mind is how well he kept his call to action clear: vote for me, tell your friends, and send money. Considering that he won the election and shattered all previous fund-raising records by bringing in more than $700 million, it seems that people responded to his calls to action.

So what were the social elements that Obama used? The very same ones your library can use in your marketing: website, blog, Facebook, Flickr, YouTube, LinkedIn, Twitter, e-mail, and mobile devices.

Obama's website served as the online headquarters for the campaign. All registered visitors had the opportunity to create their own blog where they could post their stories for their friends. They could also locate community groups and events.

The website's blog provided places for people to get detailed information about all aspects of the campaign, but the posts were designed to keep readers up to date on the latest news. It allowed for comments and provided tools to share posts. Posts included videos that were hosted from YouTube and Obama's own channel: Baracktv.com. People were invited to submit their photos and the campaign then posted them on the website.

The campaign also posted photos both on the Web and on Flickr. Videos posted to YouTube included speeches, events, and messages directly from Obama. He created a LinkedIn group where people started discussions and asked questions, and the campaign and its volunteers all took part in the conversation. He used Twitter to announce campaign and rally stops that readers could watch live via streaming video. People could also opt in for mobile and e-mail messages.

What is so amazing about Obama's campaign is that libraries can do all of the same things, maybe with the exception of paid ads (which, by the way, included television, radio, video games, and web venues).

Bring Your Library to Life with a Story

2

Why Tell a Story?

Storytelling is a powerful form of communication and learning. Compelling stories can effectively influence the attitudes, perceptions, and behaviors of your local community. Stories that do this depict transformative libraries and passionate librarians who are involved in the community and making a difference. According to the study "From Awareness to Funding," released in 2008 by the Online Computer Library Center, "Voters' attitudes, perceptions and behaviors, not their demographic profile, are the most important determinants of willingness to support increases in library funding."

Compelling stories inspire and engage people and change the way people think about things. They help people understand and make sense of what they do and why they do it. Stories can help people learn, absorb, remember, and share information.

Storytelling Is Good for Your Library

Businesses use storytelling to share their vision, sell their products, and attract the best employees. Libraries can use stories too. We can attract new members, create passionate advocates, and even reinvigorate our existing members.

Stories Help People Make Sense of Facts

People usually forget facts and figures before a conversation has even begun. A good story can paint a clear picture that allows a person to feel what you are saying, and this creates a memory that will stay with them long after they have forgotten the facts.

Stories Help Libraries Be Advocates

The ability to tell a story about an organization and the programs, products, and services it provides is essential in developing advocacy and instilling a sense of community in those who use our libraries.

- Many factors affect how people view libraries and the need for their library's funding.
- Advancements in technology have challenged the traditional value of libraries as centers for research.
- An increase in disposable income has resulted in an ownership mentality that values purchasing items over borrowing.

- A decrease in reading across the population has lowered the value of an establishment that provides free books.
- Tight budgets in municipalities have put libraries in competition for funding with such essential services as police forces.

To create support and a new vision of value, libraries need to create new stories that ring true to their communities. Stories will help you achieve that.

What Makes a Good Story?

A good story touches people. It finds the common human denominator and paints a vivid description that anyone can relate to his or her own personal experience. A good story has conflict and resolution. And most important, it is authentic and told with sincerity. A good story is also fairly short.

Are Testimonies and Stories the Same Thing?

Testimonies are written comments by satisfied customers that praise your organization and staff. Chances are that your library has collected such comments for quite a while. You may have posted them on the Web or even used them as examples of how well your library is performing. Testimonies are nice. They focus on what the library has done well or how a staff member was helpful. Stories take testimonies to the next level and show how that positive experience had an impact on a person's life.

Telling a Great Story

The easiest way to tell a great story is to break it into three phases: beginning, middle, and end. Filmmakers call this the three-act structure, and with a little adaptation of this format, you will be able to create powerful stories.

Timing

Timing is everything when it comes to telling your story. Too much time in one section will make it too slow and risk boring the listener, but not enough time will leave themes underdeveloped and can leave your listeners confused. Following an adapted three-act structure with a shorter format offers an excellent outline:

- Think of your story in four quarters.
- The first act of your story (the beginning) should make up the first quarter of the story.

- The second act of your story (the middle) should take up the next two quarters.
- The third act of your story (the ending) should make up the last quarter of the story.

So if you have eight minutes to tell your story, you'll want to spend two minutes on the beginning, four minutes on the middle, and two minutes on the ending.

Beginning: The Setup

In the beginning of the story, you can introduce the characters and briefly tell the listener what the story is about and the circumstances surrounding the action to set up the story.

- Describe the main character. This is the person who will undergo a transformation as a result of using your library. Give the listener a brief visual image of this person; share a characteristic that will help your listeners identify with this person.
- Explain why you are telling the story.
- About halfway through the beginning, introduce the specific event that causes your character to take action.
- Tell the listener about the circumstances that are driving your character to take action.
- Right before you wrap up the beginning, tell the listener that your main character has taken on a challenge to take that action. (Don't tell the outcome yet. That comes later.)

Depending on the length of your story, the beginning could be as short as thirty seconds. But it can be difficult to include all that information without running into the next section. An easy shortcut is to include brief descriptions that will let listeners quickly identify with what you are saying and let them fill in the blanks.

Set the Scene

Who could ever forget the first line of Isak Dinesen's novel *Out of Africa*: "I had a farm in Africa, at the foot of the Ngong Hills"? Well, our stories need to set the scene just like the wonderful novels you enjoy reading. The only problem is that we have only a few sentences in which to accomplish this feat.

Because you'll be talking about your community, your best bet is to use the places, phrases, and news items that the community can easily identify.

For example, "When such-and-such company laid off workers, Mary Jones was one of the fifty people who suddenly found herself without work. She never minded sacrificing her own needs, but it really hit her hard when summer rolled around and she didn't have enough money to buy the books her two children needed as part of the summer reading list their school assigned."

What are the easily identifiable events in your community? High-profile news items, popular destinations, community events, personal milestones such as anniversaries and birthdays, and increased property taxes or gas prices affect entire communities.

Middle: The Confrontation

The middle of your story tells about the obstacles the main character faces in an attempt to resolve the challenge you described in the beginning. This is where the drama develops. Ideally your character should face at least two turning points.

The first turning point should happen about a quarter through this section. For example, this might be when your character is about to achieve success but it falls apart.

The second turning point happens about midway through, when your character almost gives up hope of achieving success. For example, this might be when your character is at the lowest point and farthest away from finding resolve.

Ending: The Resolution

You've now got your listeners totally engaged. They are feeling your character's struggle. Here in the ending all those conflicts meet, and in one final moment your character finds resolve. Applause, applause!

The ending is also where you connect the dots between your character's success and the library. Don't expect that people will make the connection; you must do it for them. Include phrases such as "without the library," "because of the library," and "because the library was there."

The ending is also the place where you ask people to act. What do you want your listeners to do? Be specific. Tell them how to do what you need them to do. Should they go to a website, call the mayor, sign up for a program, check out a book? Make sure you tell them exactly what you want them to do.

Tips for Great Storytelling

1. Keep it interesting. Once you have a reader's attention you need to keep the story interesting by adding the details that will make it unusual enough to motivate people to want to read further. Compelling stories include surprising twists that distinguish the story from other stories. What makes your story different than all the others?

2. Don't forget to include one or two turning points. In motivational stories the main character should overcome an obstacle that leads him or her to certain specific actions. Conflict creates the drama that moves a story along and gives meaning to the character's actions. The obstacles don't always have to be enormous, but they do need to be identifiable. Think of the conflicts your customers face in their lives. Who can say that they have enough time in the day? But combine the conflict with an important assignment. For example, a businessperson whose computer crashed in the morning is waiting for an essential document for a proposal she is presenting, or a person who doesn't own a computer needs to fill out online applications for a job. Conflicts such as overcoming poverty, despair, or frustration are fairly generic and apply to a larger audience. The greater the conflict, the more rewarding is the successful outcome.

3. Connect with your audience by creating an authentic emotional experience. When your audience completes the journey with your character, they will have shared that experience. It is important to keep this journey authentic or else you'll risk breaking the audience's trust. It is always tempting to put on a better spin, to add a little overstatement, or to stretch the story to fit your needs, but the first rule of a good motivational story is to keep it authentic.

4. Keep it real. Don't try to turn a heartwarming story into a tragedy. Sometimes obstacles are small and personal. When they are told well, your audience will identify with the story, and that's what you want.

5. Make sure that the message of the story supports your library. If it doesn't, you might not be telling the right story. If you are working to create a word-of-mouth movement, the message of the story could become the piece that gets communicated from person to person, so don't be afraid to create a catchy phrase for it.

Stories for WOMM

People love to share stories, which are a vital element of effective WOMM. Chances are, though, that people will not tell your story the same way you did. They'll embellish some parts and forget details in other parts. If you are telling a story you hope will be shared, make sure that you start and end with a connection to your library. Keep the story line simple and don't use too many details. For example, if you tell your story at a meeting, include a written version as a handout. It could be on an index card. The Maryland State Department of Education designed postcards with photos of the people they have helped, and each postcard featured that person's story. Postcards are cheap to print, and you can design a different card for each story. You can keep the design as simple as a photo and text.

Iowa's Telling the Library Story Tool Kit

The Iowa Library Service Areas and the State Library of Iowa created the Telling the Library Story Tool Kit (available at www.silo.lib.ia.us/for-ia-libraries/tell-library-story/index.html) to assist Iowa libraries in explaining and demonstrating the value of their services in order to increase use of and support for libraries. Whether you need a bookmark, a template for an annual report, or suggestions for talking with policy makers, this comprehensive site has what you need.

Beyond Words

The Vancouver Public Library conducted a story contest a few years back and received more than 350 stories about their libraries. The stories are still posted online at www.beyondwords.ca. The following two paragraphs set the stage for a poignant story and demonstrate how powerful a story can be:

Walter Ernst 1931–2005

In late February 2005 my Father, Walter Ernst, began to take the business of dying more seriously than he had before. Or perhaps those tall dark feathered angels that surround all of us finally took more notice of him. Either way the end result was the same. And I quickly found myself sitting beside his bed while he spent nine days leaving the world.

As we neared the end of the shadowy stages of dying my Mother dropped a piece of paper on my lap. It was a simple request to write an essay on the impact of Public Libraries in one's life. That night we again sat and talked around my Father's bed. We spoke about the libraries here in British Columbia and the books that have shaped us.

> **Everyone is always talking about how libraries have changed or how valuable we are to a community, but when push comes to shove, stories about real people are the ones that will make your point.**

Story Banks

Story banks are collections of stories that an organization can use for their advocacy, promotional, and media efforts. Your organization probably already has a stack of "can we quote you" or similar complimentary statements from your customers with a line or two about how happy people were with a service you provided. That's a good beginning, but what if the media calls looking for a story about how your library is helping teens, or what if the mayor wants a specific example of how your library is helping seniors? To be truly effective, you need a method of collecting stories that includes contact information.

The Southeast Library System in Minnesota collects stories on its web page as part of its advocacy efforts. The library tells its customers why it needs the stories and how it will use them. It also provides a simple online form. Here is the library's request, from www.selco.info/resources-for-libraries/advocacy/:

We need your story! Tell us how the public library has helped you and/or your family. These stories are to be compiled in a statewide brochure that will be distributed to the people who decide on library funding issues. By filling out this form, you agree to have your name, home library, and county listed in the brochure. However, not all stories will be included in the brochure due to space limitations. If you are you willing to speak with legislators about the value of your public library, then please list your contact information below (home address, phone and/or e-mail). Your contact information will be used only for this purpose. Thanks for Being a Contributor to Our Statewide Collection of Library Stories!

Steps to Creating a Story Bank

Before you create a story bank, take some time to think about how you will use the stories—to advocate for financial support, to promote a service, to create a buzz online, to bring more people into your library, to get more people to go to your website, to use on promotional materials, to pitch stories to the media or respond to stories from the media. Knowing how you will use the stories will help you decide what kind of information you'll collect, how to store that information, and how often you need to update the stories.

1. **Create a story-bank web page and link to it from your homepage.** The page should tell what the story bank is, why you are collecting stories, and any parameters you've established for sharing the stories.

2. **Create an online form.** It is important to be able to speak with the people who offer you their stories. You may need to obtain additional information, update the story, or call to ask if a reporter can contact the storyteller directly.

The form should include essential basic information: name, address, phone number, e-mail, and an area for the person to type in the story. Other questions you may want to include are the following:

- May we publish your name in connection with your story?
- May we use all or part of your story (or share it with library support organizations) in marketing, publicity, or fund-raising efforts?

3. **Keep the stories up to date.** To be effective, stories need to be authentic and timely. People move; their experiences change. Ideally, you should periodically update your stories, but if time is an issue, make sure that you call the person before using the story.

Stories for Advocacy: Solving Life's Problems

Nancy pulled together a marketing and advocacy campaign for the New Jersey State Library and the New Jersey Library Association using oral, written, and multimedia stories. In the first year, they're holding a contest to encourage libraries to collect stories from their customers, create story banks, and produce multimedia productions of those stories. Libraries are being provided with a manual and training opportunities. In the second year the State Library and the New Jersey Library Association plan to use the stories for a statewide marketing and advocacy campaign. The manual and details of the campaign are posted online at www.solvinglifesproblems.org.

Story banks are crucial elements of advocacy campaigns. Politicians always want stories from their constituents. Including the addresses of those who provide stories makes it easy for you to select the appropriate story.

Quick List of Questions to Guide Your Story Contributors

- What's your most memorable experience at the library?
- Why do you visit the library?
- What have you learned at the library?
- How have librarians helped you?
- How does the library save you money?
- How has the library changed your life?
- What would your life be like if you didn't have your library?
- What is the best class you've ever taken at the library?
- What is the best program you ever attended at the library?
- Did you discover a book at one of our public libraries that changed the way you look at the world and your place in it?
- Did you meet someone significant at the library?
- Did something amusing make your day?

The Multnomah County Library: Guiding Customers to Tell Their Stories

The Multnomah County Library in Oregon includes specific questions to guide people in telling their stories. You can use this concept to gather stories for specific programs, services, or initiatives that you want to support or promote.

A selection of Multnomah County Library stories will be posted on this website and may also be used in other promotional materials. So, tell us:

- What's your most memorable experience at the library?

- Has a library book changed your life?

- Why do you visit the library?

- Why does Multnomah County Library deserve everyone's support?

- What have you learned at the library?

- How have librarians helped you?

- What's *your* story?

The Multnomah Library collected quite a few stories. I can envision the following story as a centerpiece of any presentation, but can you imagine the impact it might have when told to a group of potential funders?

> I have an autoimmune disease. What this means is that I can't leave the house by myself and I can't do very much. I spend a lot of time in bed and there are only a few activities I can still do. But my love of reading has sustained me. Since I can't work I don't have money so the library has become a huge resource for me. I can put several books on hold at once and send my mom to get them for me or pick them up when I have a doctor's appointment. In other's stories I can escape my illness and experience theirs for a while. Thank you so much for your online catalog; without it, my life would be much less thrilling.
>
> Anonymous Library: Hollywood

How to Market Electronic Resources

3

Libraries' reference collections, periodicals, and more and more monograph collections are increasingly being delivered electronically. This shift in delivery drastically changes the footprint of a library. We are used to being storehouses of thousands or millions of volumes of books, almanacs, encyclopedias, dictionaries, and journals. Beyond the physical changes this shift brings, it also changes the ways we market these resources. Sometimes it feels that we are marketing the invisible.

How Do We Connect Users with Electronic Resources?

- Try to relate the librarian to electronic resources in some way, such as by using pictures and a combination of print and electronic marketing.
- Create an electronic resource page that has your liaison's picture and contact information.
- Make a library trading card with a list of electronic resources that your liaison can offer to help with.
- Make a MOO card (at www.moo.com—cheap and cool full-color business cards).
- Make a bookmark that highlights electronic resources.
- Create an online newsletter that people can subscribe to that updates patrons about new databases and other electronic resources of interest.

Always make sure that the help regarding your electronic resources is embedded into each page. Patrons will never have to leave the page if they run into a problem or need more information. Rather than put up barriers, you will create communication points.

Types of help include the following:

- Reference phone number
- Embedded chat service
- E-mail for reference services
- Contact information to report a technical problem
- Link to sign up for research consultation

Clean up that laundry list of databases—oh heck, throw it out completely! A new way to think of ourselves as collection development librarians is to pick the top three databases in a subject area and give quick explanations geared toward your target audiences for each database.

Do Not Cut and Paste the Vendor's Explanation of a Database!

Here is an example of copied-and-pasted text from a vendor for Academic Search Premier:

> Provides full text for 4,486 publications (3,718 peer-reviewed) covering academic areas of study including social sciences, humanities, education, computer sciences, engineering, language and linguistics, arts and literature, medical sciences, and ethnic studies. A total of 8,204 titles are abstracted and indexed, of which 7,132 are peer-reviewed.

This is just too much information and too many details. Remember that vendors are selling databases to your library, so they are trying to impress you, the librarian. We care about how many articles are indexed, but patrons care only about the article they want.

Making the description connect to your audience doesn't have to be time consuming. Just write it as a benefit statement. The trick to writing the benefit statement is answering the question, "Why would your customers use this?"

Benefit Statement

A benefit statement is all about keeping the user in mind. Ask yourself what problems users could solve with your resource. But don't stop there! Go from good to great with your benefit statements.

+ A good benefit statement:

    "This scholarly database contains more than 3,600 peer-reviewed publications in full-text on every subject."

+ A great benefit statement:

    "Academic Search Premier: A great place to begin your research! It covers all subject areas and contains mostly full-text scholarly and popular articles."

Bringing It All Home

Don't worry about the delivery method—push the content! That is what patrons care about. Find ways to tell your audience about electronic collections that will be of direct interest to them.

+ Having a music program? Tell them about audio streaming.
+ Having a history lecture? Tell them about historical newspapers or streaming video of famous speeches.
+ Hosting an art exhibit? Tell them about image databases.

Take advantage of having your target audience in front of you and give them specific content to connect to.

Your Databases Provide Rich Content

Electronic resources are notoriously hard to market, especially for nonacademic librarians, because the direct benefit may not be tied to getting a great grade in class.

Think of imaginative ways that your audience can use your electronic resources.

- Someone who is writing a book might need public domain images.
- Someone who is making a video might need public domain music.
- An amateur who is going pro and publishing might need to explore your electronic resources.

Marketing Resources through Wikipedia

Solve the Wikipedia problem once and for all! We can use our rich resources to make Wikipedia richer.

....

Right now the dominant user-generated site for combined search is Wikipedia, but that may change in the future.

....

There are many benefits to marketing your resources through Wikipedia:

- Use Google Analytics to prove to funders that patrons are using your digitized collection.
- Help ensure future investment in digitization.
- Meet customers where they are.
- Create a reach well beyond your own catalog.
- Raise the profile of your entire institution.
- Have your resources show up higher in web search results.

The major issue to be aware of when marketing your resources through Wikipedia is the fact that the maintenance process is very time consuming. Someone may edit out your resources at any time, so you need to keep a watch over the pages that incorporate your resources.

Make sure that you have set up a succession plan for monitoring and incorporating your resources into Wikipedia. This way, no matter who takes over the job of maintaining the entries, that person can pick up where the previous employee left off.

Bridging Print to Electronic

Create very specific bookmarks with the top three databases (specially tailored to each of your target audiences).

Work with your IT department to create more intuitive URLs. There is nothing worse than seeing www.library.something.edu/8085/database_list/resources/wdex.html, when that address could easily be www.library.something.edu/databases/.

If working with IT is a problem, try TinyURL.com. You just type in a long URL, and with a push of a button, you will receive a new shorter URL. The site also offers you the ability to customize your links with keywords and to view page-traffic statistics. All of this is free.

Create business cards with electronic resources on the front and contact information on the back. Everyone carries a wallet—students, businesspeople, people studying abroad.

Things to remember when negotiating with your database providers:

+ Make sure that you can embed your logo into each database page.
+ Ask them to provide you with talking points to help sell databases for each specific target audience.
+ Ask them to provide high-resolution images that you can use in marketing materials.
+ Ask them for templates that you can customize.
+ Ask before you buy—try to negotiate before you write the check.
+ Ask them to provide a marketing plan and tools to help you promote the databases to your customers.

Federated Search

Most library usability studies of the past five years have shown that customers feel overwhelmed by the amount of search results that a federated search returns. A better way to use your federated search is to narrow the amount of databases per subject area and allow customers to add databases as they see fit. This way customers will end up with only relevant results. Gettysburg College has done a great job of this (see http://libguides.gettysburg.edu/visualarts/).

The New Collection Management

Use your subject expertise to choose databases that are relevant to your community. Make sure you know the insides of those databases like you used to know the breadth of your print collection.

The majority of academic libraries have honed the process of selecting databases, and this can serve as a model for other libraries:

- Research new options for databases.
- Pick several that seem appropriate for the subject area.
- Provide demonstrations to the faculty in that subject area and allow trial subscriptions.
- Ask faculty to provide feedback to librarians.
- Gather recommendations and make the final decision.
- Purchase the database.
- Work with faculty to integrate the new database into the curriculum.

The benefit of being an academic library in this situation is that the customers have clearly defined roles and the community is usually finite, but this can still serve as a model for other types of libraries.

Summary: Marketing Electronic Resources

- ☐ Create a connection between the electronic resource and the librarian.
- ☐ Embed help into each electronic resource page.
- ☐ Pick the top three databases for each subject area.
- ☐ Use events and programs to highlight a targeted electronic resource.
- ☐ Push the rich content of your databases.
- ☐ Market your electronic resources through Wikipedia.
- ☐ Find ways to bridge electronic to print.

Public Relations 101

4

Be the Press

You can make your media releases work for your library with or without being published by your local newspapers. Of course coverage by the traditional press still has its advantages. News coverage still earns the attention from communities and important stakeholders such as your board members.

Everyone is right in saying that newspapers aren't the only go-to medium and it's important to spread out where and to whom you distribute your information, but we are finding that many people still rely on their local newspaper for library news. Anything we can do to stay visible in all mediums can only be to our advantage.

—Manuela Miracle, *Public Relations Office, Somerset County Library System*

The New-Media Mix

The new generation of library customers gets news from websites and blogs. To get maximum exposure for your programs, products, or services, take a three-pronged approach to reach traditional and new-media readers:

+ Send information to news outlets.
+ Post press releases on your website.
+ Create an interesting tidbit on your blog that links to your media releases.

One avenue that I used extensively when I worked in public libraries was to develop a relationship with the newspaper photographer. Sounds crazy but it's a great way to connect with the newspaper and often he would call me looking for a good photo opportunity. This often led to a follow-up story. The photographer I worked with had young children so I would always let him know when there was something neat going on at the library that I thought his children might enjoy. This relationship led to some very good newspaper coverage.

—Pam Jaskot, *library consultant for communications, State Library of North Carolina*

Strategies for the New Media

Content is king, and with the onslaught of new websites and blogs looking for information to fill their sites, your news might be gold to the right site. That means that somewhere someone might consider news almost anything that is happening at your library.

Photos are content. If you post your photos online, be sure to give them complete titles and descriptions. Make sure you also post your photos to your social networks and blogs.

Press Release Newswires

Newswires like PR Newswire and Business Wire not only get your releases out to major publications but also are able to get your releases to online news services—a nice plus. The negative side is that such services cost money. A quick search will give you lists of wire services that can fit every budget. If you are just looking to land a spot on news services like Google and Yahoo!, you can go with a basic press release distribution service, but the costs are still in the hundreds of dollars per release. On a tight budget you might do better creating your own media list and letting the RSS feeds go to work on your blog.

It is important to make personal contacts with each of your media outlets (editor, news director, publisher)—that way, if you really want to push something, you know who to contact and they know who to contact whenever they want to take the initiative on a story. To let them know how much I appreciate their promotion of our events/services during the year, I drop off a box of chocolate or cookies to five of my major sources with thank-you cards around Valentine's Day.

—Maryelle De Jong, *Danbury Library, Connecticut*

Creating a Media List

Don't be intimidated by the idea of creating a media list. In the old days we spent a lot of time developing our media lists. Nowadays reporters expect to get releases via e-mail, so for the most part, compiling huge mailing lists is overkill. An effective media list can be as simple as a list of e-mail addresses of the editors of local newspapers. Your best bet is to create an e-mail distribution list in Microsoft Outlook and add the e-mail addresses of reporters and editors. It will make it easier for you if you create a new distribution list for each type of mailing you send. For example, you might have separate distribution lists for local news, business news, and statewide news.

Creating a Media List for Staff Releases

Any news that includes accomplishments of individual staff members should be sent to their hometown newspapers as well as college alumni newsletters. The easiest way to create this type of list is to ask each staff member to send you the names of their local newspapers and contact information for their alumni association publications.

Posting Press Releases to Your Website

Create a press section on your web pages for your news releases and make sure it is linked to from every page on your site. Once the releases are posted, search engine crawlers will find the content, index it, and rank it. The higher the rank, the better are your chances of being listed on the first page when people conduct a search with Google and other search engines.

Search Engine Optimization (SEO) Tips to Achieve a Higher Ranking

- Use the main phrases and words in both the title and the article.
- Use keywords as much as naturally possible in the first paragraph.
- Use phrasing or words that match the words people would use to search for you.
- Include lots of links—crawlers count them as relevant.
- Write out the name of the links rather than "Click Here."
- Understand keywords and make sure your releases contain them.
- Insert keywords that correspond with newsworthy events.
- Create links to specific pages of your website in releases.

Writing Your Release

When you begin creating news releases, consider who would benefit the most by knowing the information, and then write your release with those readers in mind. Are you entertaining, informing, or educating them?

Use the writing style that matches your intent, but no matter what, follow these pointers:

- Make the first two sentences attention grabbing.
- Make the whole release interesting and easy to comprehend.
- Write as if you are speaking to your reader, and use plain language.
- Keep your paragraphs short.
- If you have lists, use bullet points.
- Include links to additional information on your web pages.
- Stay away from library jargon.
- Avoid acronyms.
- Write some big-picture pieces to give readers a fuller perspective on issues.

If you only rely on traditional media you are placing the success of your activity/organization in their hands. Scary thought. There is only so much space, so much time and too much news and events for them to do everything. You need to make it easy for them. Don't just send them press releases—send them everything else they need to write that story. My author promotion pitch includes a news release, reviews, links to other coverage, a book cover image, and an offer to get them a copy of the book or interview. If it is a local author [or] self-published author I put some responsibility on them to get out their friends, families, neighbors, etc.

Target your audience. Contact mountaineering groups about your book talk on mountain photography (and don't forget the photography clubs). Stay in touch not only with college communication folks, but individual college departments that share an interest. To do this, you really need to know your community. When we had Bradford Washburn here to speak about his career and his photographs (which were in our gallery) almost three hundred people attended. Not exactly a household name out West, he was a climber, a scientist, a mapmaker, a former museum director (founder of the modern Boston Museum of Science), and he pioneered the use of aerial photography in the analysis of mountains and in planning mountaineering expeditions. His photography is legendary (and mostly unknown). How did we pack the room? We identified and worked with the groups that participate in the activities he participated in.

Collaborate and cosponsor. Cross-marketing is powerful. Don't do it all by yourself when there are other organizations who could benefit by the success of your program. Just remember, collaboration works both ways.

—David Domkoski, *manager of community relations, Tacoma Public Library*

First Things First—Is It News?

While Web 2.0 tools help us promote stories to a wider audience than the one many newspapers have, there are still advantages to having a story in your local newspaper. Calendar items listing your events are easy enough to land, but when you ask the press to cover a story, the first question editors need to answer is whether it is newsworthy.

One of the harsh realities of media—especially print media—is the competition for time and space, and the relative disinterest in happy stories and good news. We're in a major media market, and if we get one or two stories a *year* in our local dailies, we've exceeded expectations. And the stories we do get aren't about events—they're about core library services. We also get excellent coverage in the Community Calendar listings. They're just the basics, but they're what the public needs. We've found our best results are to view the media as our *audience:* if we can demonstrate to them that *our* information is vital to *their* audience, they'll be as helpful as they can. I rarely ask for specific coverage—but I follow up on stories where we have a natural connection, and I feed possible features to the specific contact most likely to carry it. It helps to target your reporters/editors very carefully, and give them what they need, in the format they want, when they need it most. If in doubt, ask them—when you want nothing in return.

—Marsha Iverson, *public relations specialist, King County Library System, Washington*

Timing

The concept of timing is where the whole concept of news comes from. Is your story new, or is there new information that readers will want to know about? Something may be very interesting today, but tomorrow it is yesterday's news and papers won't want to run it.

Importance

How many people will the story affect? If you try to get coverage for an event that you know will attract a large number of readers, make sure you tell that to the reporters.

Proximity

Stories that happen within the newspaper's distribution mean more to editors. This is especially relevant for local newspapers. Help editors make the connection by naming the town where you are located, where the event will take place, or where your employee resides.

VIPs

Famous people get more coverage just because they are famous. If a congressional representative, senator, mayor, or a local or national star is coming, make sure the reporter knows! On the other hand, if that person cancels, you should take the time to let the reporter know. Relationships with reporters are developed over time and require trust.

Human Interest

Editors always welcome human-interest stories that emotionally appeal to readers. There is a thin line between a human-interest story and an infomercial, but reporters can spot the difference from a mile away! Remember to keep the story about human interest and let your library play the supporting role.

How to Send Your Release

Before you decide on a format for your release, decide whether you will e-mail or fax it. The only way to know which is best is to call the media outlet and ask how it prefers to get releases. E-mail is a fairly standard mode of operating, but there are still places that prefer a fax.

Deadline

For the most part, for news releases, newspapers like a two-week lead time for events and a two- to three-week lead time for public service announcements.

News Release Format

Use the inverted-pyramid style to place important information first:

+ The first sentence is the hook.
+ The first paragraph should include who, what, where, when, & why.
+ Try to include a quote in every other paragraph.
+ Keep an active voice.
+ Include photographs whenever possible—but attach them; don't paste them in.

Attachments

If you have more that you want the reporter to know, you can add attachments to your release.

Backgrounders

Some articles require that a reporter conduct additional research to write the article. In those cases, it is helpful to send backgrounders with in-depth information that is comprehensive but concise. This is great when you want a reporter to have lots of information about the opening of a new library or comprehensive programs.

- Open with a concise statement of an issue or subject.
- Use subheadings for each section so the reporter can easily find information.
- Follow with a historical overview of the issue or subject—be factual.
- Work your way to the present.
- Explain the implications of the issue.

Fact Sheets

Fact sheets present just the facts—use charts, headings, or bullet points that the reporter can use for the story.

Links to Websites and Blogs

Let the reporter know what is available at the sites, but make sure you've checked the addresses first. Nothing is worse than sending a reporter to a dead link or a site that hasn't been updated.

Photos

Label all photos with the type of file and a caption. For example, "JPEG Mrs. Smith can be seen performing with the Rolling Stones at the Let's Eat Cake concert sponsored by the Anytown Library."

How to Write a Traditional News Release

If you are sending a release to a news agency, you'll want to use media standards. Traditional press releases are written in an inverted-pyramid style with the most important information in the first paragraph. Ideally the release should be written so that an editor can edit from the bottom paragraph by paragraph without losing the essential information.

Common Parts of Press Releases

ID block: Placed on the upper left side of your press release, write the word *news* in all caps and bold. If you're not using letterhead, make sure you put the name and address of your library here.

Contacts: Name, phone number, and e-mail. Hint—include two names to make sure the reporter can always reach someone.

For immediate release: The standard title for a release date is "For Immediate Release" in all caps. You may omit this line, but always include the date.

Dateline: This tells the reader the town where the reporter gathered the basic information for the story. Begin your release with a dateline by typing the name of your town in caps followed by a dash.

Headline: Headline writing is an art in itself. Headlines need to be succinct and informative and convey a message while captivating the reporter's attention, all in about eight words. The best way to develop headline-writing skills is to spend time reading headlines of the company you're submitting your stories to.

Boilerplate: Libraries can create a short paragraph that describes the organization, products, services, and mission statement for placement at the end of the release.

Slug: If your release runs more than one page, write the word *more* in brackets or between dashes, centered at the bottom of the first page.

Slug line: This is a description of the article in italics followed by dashes then page number, such as "Librarian of the year—page 2."

End of release: The end of the release is designated with "End" or "30" in quotes or "###."

The first sentence is considered the hook. You'll need to catch the reader's attention or risk that he or she will move on to another article. That first paragraph must answer the who, what, where, when, and why about the story.

Try to include a quote in every other paragraph. Choose to quote the people in your organization who are relevant to the story. The best way to get interesting quotes is to ask for a specific subject to be covered in the quote. It often helps if you write up a draft of the talking points you are looking for the person to include in a quote. Always advise people to give quotes that reflect their personality rather than an alter ego. Authenticity is always the best approach.

Include photographs whenever possible—attach them as JPEGs; don't paste them in the e-mail. If it is the first time you are sending an attachment, check with the reporter to find out his or her preference.

The Media Advisory

Many librarians automatically create a full press release when a simple media advisory or photo op would do. If you are looking to get a reporter or photographer to cover an event, you can save yourself some time by using the following format.

MEDIA ADVISORY
Name of Library, Street, City, State, and Zip Code

NEWS RELEASE [month, date, year]

Contacts: [List the names, e-mail, and phone numbers of people the reporter can call for more information. It's a good idea to include a second contact of someone who will be at the library when you aren't there.]

MEDIA ADVISORY/Photo Op

[If you are just requesting a photographer, replace "Media Advisory" with "Photo Op."]

Who: [List the notables who are attending the event.]

What: [Write one or two sentences summarizing the event.]

When: [Include the date and time.]

Where: [Include the name of the place and fill in the address.]

Details: [Include a short paragraph that explains why the event is newsworthy.]

###

[The three hash marks signal the end of the release.]

What Kind of Release Should You Send?

Although it would be nice if everything we did rated a full-page feature story, it doesn't. The best way to understand what kind of release you should send is by looking at your newspaper, comparing those stories to yours, and noting what kind of coverage they received.

Did they receive a couple of paragraphs (blurb), a half- to full-page article, an article with a picture, a picture with a deep caption, or a calendar listing? These are good indicators of how an editor would feature your story as well.

Type of coverage: Blurb and community calendar listing

> **Type of release:** Media advisory—an alert to the media of an upcoming event or story that is relevant to the media's audience. This is a straightforward release that lists who, what, when, where, and why.

Type of coverage: Picture with deep caption, feature story

> **Type of release:** Photo-op request—an alert to the media about a photo opportunity. If you think this is something that can be expanded to include a feature story, then make sure you include a full release. If it's just a photo and caption, then describe why this would make a good picture opportunity and include directions to the event.

Type of coverage: News or feature story

> **Type of release:** News release—you have a great event or a news item and it covers two, three, or even four criteria that editors look for in a story. A larger daily paper will use your news release as a base for an article, but most daily papers will pop a staff byline on it and publish it in full.

One thing we've started with lately is having some trusted volunteers enter in information into all of the online calendars, which can be tedious and a time drainer. One of our programmers at a branch started this effort and makes sure the information is correct on the websites. It's helping her promote her programs because we just don't have the time to do it.

—Robin Klaene, *public relations director, Kenton Library, Kentucky*

Headlines

Well-written headlines are the essence of the news point of a story. They are positive and specific; they contain strong, active verbs and short, simple words.

A great headline on a press release

- Grabs attention
- Leads the reporters into the story and makes them want to read more
- Helps the reporter understand the story without reading the entire article
- Saves the reporter the time of having to rewrite a new headline

Some hints to writing good headlines:

- Use present tense.
- Use an active voice, which saves words by using the subject and verb together.
- Use short, to-the-point words.
- Make positive statements (e.g., "No funding for libraries" versus "Legislature keeps library budget flat").
- Omit articles and avoid abbreviations, exclamation points, and other punctuation.
- Use important numbers only. Except for one, all numbers in headlines should be written as numerals.

Basic AP Style

Associated Press (AP) style is the standard for newspapers. By using AP style, you exhibit professionalism and make reporters' jobs much easier, allowing them to just cut and paste your story without having to edit it.

Listing Events

Time—date—building—street—town

The event will take place 4 p.m., March 1, at the Anytown Public Library, 123 Main Street, Anytown.

If you include the day, then use

Time—day—date—building—street—town

The event will take place 4 p.m., Tuesday, March 1, at the Anytown Public Library, 123 Main Street, Anytown.

Be sure to add periods on a.m. and p.m.—nothing will drive the reporter to tears more than having to go through a listing filled with times that he or she has to go through and add periods to, especially when they are on deadline!

Abbreviations

Before a full name outside a direct quote, abbreviate the following: Dr., Gov., Lt. Gov., Mr., Mrs., Ms., Rep., Rev., Sen.

Inside a direct quote, spell out all except Dr., Mr., Mrs., and Ms.

After a name abbreviate Jr. or Sr.

After the name of a corporate entity, abbreviate Co., Inc., and Ltd.

Sending Your Release through E-mail

- When using e-mail, try to keep pertinent information visible in the first screen.
- Use the subject line to inform and attract reporters.
- Attach JPEGs and include captions.

Press Releases Don't Always Have to Be about an Event

Here are some examples of press releases that every library should send or post to their online newsletter:

- Awards for both the organization and all staff members
- New promotions or acceptance to unique or exclusive organizations
- Speeches at national or international events
- Appointments to boards or task forces
- A new service or product that provides a solution to a problem (the product or service isn't as important as how it will solve a problem for the reader)

A Note about Releases for New Services

While we may consider new services important news, newspapers may not necessarily agree. So the alternative approach is to write the release for web posting only. That means dropping the AP style and writing your release to appeal to the reader. Keep your posts short and add photos for interest.

Two Tips about Keywords

If you are going to post your news items to the Web, you need to make sure you have included metatags and keywords to ensure that search engines pick up your articles. While there are tons of books written on search engine optimization (SEO), there are two simple SEO tips you can use for your news items:

- Include your keywords in your title.
- When you include links, write out the name of the link rather than "Click Here."

Get Better Results from Your Releases

- Upload your photos to Flickr and share links with reporters.
- Are you making news? Be the iReporter—submit photos and videos to the CNN website and local news sites.
- Establish your expertise with reporters. Create a list of the staff's areas of expertise with e-mail and phone numbers and post it online. You can also send the list to your local newspapers.
- If you can't land a story, write about it in a letter to the editor.

> We have relationships with a couple of local radio stations, and we record PSAs each month that they run. It's free and we can write our own copy.
>
> —Linda Avellar, *communications supervisor, Ferguson Library, Connecticut*

Public Service Announcements—PSAs

General Guidelines for PSAs

A PSA is any unpaid announcement that promotes voluntary, government or nonprofit organizations, or other programs. After the Federal Communication Commission deregulated the rules in the 1980s, allowing stations to determine their own standards for public interest programming, it was difficult to get on the air. But there is renewed interest at the FCC that could result in more airtime. For example, satellite radio might be required to provide public interest programming. With that in mind, it may be worth your library's time to look into adding PSAs to your media mix.

- The best way to get on the air is to have a relationship with the radio station. It would be worth your time to visit the station manager in person to update his or her perception of what your library does for the community. Don't be overwhelming. Start with the most appealing services, and then add more information as you develop the relationship.

- For stations with larger broadcast areas, it would be beneficial to collaborate with surrounding libraries for general interest announcements, such as summer reading, Banned Books Week, National Library Week, and so on.
- Include only pertinent information when you send your PSA to the station.
- Attach a brief letter of introduction explaining the announcement to enhance its chances of being aired. Include your library's name, address, contact person's name, and phone number.
- Allow a lead time of two to three weeks for maximum effect.
- Tailor your PSA to the station's listening audience.
- Thirty-second announcements are played most often, but prepare ten- or fifteen-second announcements to be used as fillers.
- Be sure the scripts are easy to read and have no tongue-twisting language.
- Include your website's URL.
- Type in all caps and use double spacing.

We use free podcasting software (Audacity) and an inexpensive microphone (from your local Wal-Mart, etc.). We put together monthly PSAs for our message-on-hold on our phone system and also send them to our local radio station who plays them for us. It is a lot of fun!

—Amie Thomas, *public services administrator, Brownsburg Public Library, Indiana*

Word-Count Estimates for On-Air Time

- 10 seconds—25 words
- 20 seconds—40 words
- 30 seconds—80 words
- 60 seconds—160 words

A trick of the trade? It is easier to add than to take away!

Outreach

A librarian we knew had the task of trying to bring young adults into her library. The library was new, spacious, and ready for a flood of YA customers. The problem was the YA section was totally underused. Like any good outreach librarian, she decided to go where the teens were. Not to school but to the soccer field, which just happened to be right next to the library. She didn't set up a table or put out a banner; she simply sat down next to parents, introduced herself, and suggested that their children might be interested in attending a particular program and handed them a flier. Does it sound too easy? Well, what really helped was that she took the time to create programs that would interest young soccer players and offered them at a time when there were no games or practice. In other words, she did her homework. When it comes to outreach, that is one of the key ingredients to success.

Successful outreach begins with two simple questions:

1. Why are you going?
2. What do you want to achieve?

Defining exactly why you want to go on an outreach is essential. Once you know why you are going, then ask yourself what you want to accomplish with the outreach. Be specific with your answer. The librarian looking to get teens into her library saw her outreach as the first step to filling her library. By going to the soccer field she was looking to get a certain amount of teens to a specific program. But it was the first step of a larger plan to meet her goals. Once she got the kids there, she immediately started to empower them by asking them what kind of programs they wanted. And then she followed through and offered those programs. She also made sure that all the teens signed up with e-mail for the next program before they left, and she used e-mail to remind them of the program. She eventually developed a very active teen advisory board that ran the programs. But everything began with a very simple outreach.

Outreach doesn't have to be complicated, and it doesn't have to involve meeting hundreds of people at once. Effective outreach begins with a purpose and then grows into a plan.

Trade Shows

Trade shows and expos offer opportunities to meet small businesses from specific industries, administrators, educators, politicians, and even reporters. While the large shows may cost too much for your budget, smaller local shows can help you meet face-to-face with target audiences that might not be walking into your library.

The problem with trade shows is that the format is geared to generate leads that a sales team will use after the show to follow up and close a deal. Because many librarians are uncomfortable with the sales process, they use their time at shows as a networking opportunity and never really get the full benefits of the venue.

One of the costliest mistakes libraries make is to pay for a table when all they really want to do is network with the attendees. If you want to meet a few people from the industry, you can save yourself a lot of money and time by just attending a show. As an attendee you have some terrific opportunities to network not only with vendors but also with others who are attending. Bring lots of business cards, and be sure to make those follow-up phone calls to further engage in networking.

There are many circumstances in which libraries can benefit from the trade-show venue at a conference or expo, but you need know exactly why you are going and set up your table or booth to give you those results. The following five steps will help you get there.

Five Steps to a Successful Show

1. Set goals.
2. Design the booth.
3. Create simple and cheap promotional materials.
4. Train staff.
5. Follow up.

Set Measurable Goals

Setting measurable goals is the most crucial step to your success. What do you want people to know or do as a result of visiting your table? Be specific. The beauty of a trade show is that your target audience is predefined. So ask yourself what you want to achieve. Here are some common reasons:

+ Building awareness for the library
+ Introducing something new
+ Explaining a new technology
+ Motivating people to try a product
+ Gathering information

Once you decide on the purpose, make it measurable. How many people do you want to sign up for a mailing list? How many business cards do you want from people who would like to get more information about a program? Try to keep your numbers reasonable. Start with a 1 percent response rate.

Develop Key Messages

A key message is the piece of information you want your visitors to remember when they leave your table. It should be one sentence and easy to remember. An example of a key message for libraries might be, "The library has just launched a new small business center." Keep it short and sweet.

The secondary message adds another bit of information, such as "The small business center is conducting professional workshops and training sessions on an ongoing basis."

Notice that we did not use the word *free*. Everyone knows that libraries offer free programs. Your key messages need to include what people don't know. What the small business owner probably doesn't know is that the programs are professional and ongoing.

How Many Key Messages Should You Have for an Outreach?

Libraries have so many products, programs, and services that it can be difficult to choose one or two things to talk about, but doing so is essential. Your visitors are only human and can take in only a certain amount of information. When they are bombarded with lists of information, they usually stop listening and begin vigorously nodding their heads to get away as fast as they can. That doesn't mean you can't answer a question if asked, but if you have a clear purpose for the outreach, it should be relatively easy to select a key message that emphasizes the outcome you are looking to achieve.

Design the Booth

A standard booth is ten feet by ten feet. The theories behind booth design are all about getting people to go where you need them to go. The most successful designs invite people into the space while creating a flowing pattern to guide them through the booth. Imagine the booth as a line at Disneyland and each step along the way has something inviting to participate in. One of the best booth arrangements we ever saw was hosted by a major medical insurance carrier. It had five stations set up, and each one highlighted a specific service. Each section had a really neat giveaway, like sunscreen, a pedometer, vitamins, and so on. As people approached a section, the expert would chat for a few minutes (expressing the company's talking points), give away a sample of the product, and then invite visitors to chat with the next person. The thing about these giveaways was that they were actual products, not cheap items with a brand imprint. For the most part, the booth worked because the company trained the staff to make sure everyone was on message. You don't have to be as elaborate as that, but consider how people will enter and exit your booth. Try to separate activities. If you are showing people a video, where do they go after they've watched it?

An easy setup is to place two tables on either side of the booth and to leave the middle open. That way people interact on the sides. If they want to have a conversation, you can pull them toward the middle and avoid a traffic jam. If you can afford it, order a café table with high bar stools so the people who are manning the booth can rest while still inviting people to the booth. Sometimes we just place a chair at the entrance off to the side so that staff can rest and still greet visitors.

Design Your Table

You have about four seconds to attract people to look at your table and, if you're lucky, another two seconds to reel them in.

A well-designed table will help you attract your target audience so you'll be able to engage them in a quick conversation to get the information you need to follow up after the conference. Do not try to engage people in long conversations!

Create an experience, make it memorable, and tell them you'll follow up with more information, a meeting, an invitation to join your online newsletter, and so on.

A table or booth at a trade show serves as a first introduction to lots and lots of people who you can contact again. Even if you are demonstrating a new service or product, the table is a place where you can wow them, but it will be with the follow-up contact that you close the deal.

Key Elements for Any Table

+ Signage
+ Interactivity
+ Giveaways
+ Print materials

when the booth is empty, but if there are large crowds, lingering guests can work against your goals. It is a good idea to make sure that everyone working the booth knows what is expected ahead of time. It is important to designate different roles to help the staff move crowds and put them in touch with the people they need to meet. For example, designate one person to engage in longer discussions, answer questions in depth, or even provide on online demonstration. When staff meet someone who needs more time, they can walk the guest over to the designated staff person, make the introductions, and go back to greeting more people.

Table Tips

- Never sit behind your table. If you need to sit, set up chairs off to the side and lean on them.
- Try getting rid of the standard table and replace it with a small cocktail table.
- Don't chase or call out to people to get them to your booth.
- Take lots of pictures and post to Flickr.
- Create simple and cheap promotional materials, and forget about those small giveaways!
- The best promotional item for any expo is the business card.
- Don't use your expensive brochures, because they will just get thrown away along with all the other hundreds of brochures attendees collected during the day.

Follow Up

When the conference is over, the work really begins!

- Post photos to Flickr.
- Write a press release for your online newsletter with a link to the photos.
- Send a deep-caption release (i.e., a photo with a long caption) to your local paper.
- Follow up on all those contacts.
- Enter the e-mail addresses in your mailing list.
- Send an e-mail announcing that you've added them to your mailing list with a link to the photos. Include a paragraph that explains that you intend to use the photos in your newsletters or other

publications. Ask them to notify you if they don't want you to use the photos.

- Let them know that they can use photos of themselves in their newsletters, but ask them to list the photo credit for your library.
- If you received comments or suggestions at the conference, mention them on your blog or website.
- Post a photo to your website and link to the full set from the event.

Image Is Everything

Does your table reflect the image you want to convey? At a conference, we once met a financial planner. The table had a few plastic piggy banks and a sign made out of loose-leaf paper offering an opportunity to win a free prize in exchange for business cards. All we kept thinking was, Who in the world would trust that man with their money when he couldn't even plan ahead for this event? If you are claiming to be the greatest place for teens, then make sure your table would fit right in with MTV. If you are trying to attract businesses, wear a suit and set up a table that has a professional feel.

Detailing Your Brand

Where does it make sense to put your brand? You've got your brand in all the typical places: on your literature, posters, and banners. Take a few minutes to see whether there's an unexpected place to reinforce your message. At one conference Staples had a Skee-Ball game. It had pasted its "Easy" button to the start button and voilà—fun, eye-catching branding.

Taking Why to Wow!

It doesn't take a lot of money to create an outstanding table. You want to create an appealing experience, and creativity can make up for a lack of money. You can get some fantastic ideas by looking at store windows in big cities. Even if you can't get to a big city, there are plenty of photos and videos posted online.

We loved the booth that Jersey City set up when it was promoting the city as a cultural oasis at a statewide conference. They brought the outdoors in with a tent canopy, palm trees, large pictures of community members, and a wide-screen monitor playing a video with shots of the city. The giveaways were bottles of Jersey City water and miniature palm trees. They could have probably saved money on the palm trees, but the water idea was perfect. Creativity wins over big budgets that produce boring booths. It was amazing how that tent set the whole booth apart from everyone else.

Here are a few other neat ideas:

- Set up an interview atmosphere to look like a TV talk show and interview people about their experiences attending the conference.
- Re-create a popular TV game show with your library as a theme and invite people to participate.
- Create a booth highlighting the library as a green resource. Use recycled books to make furniture.

Outreach: The Why Matters—A Worksheet

Planning

The most important aspect of conducting outreach is to know why you are doing it. Begin by answering the following questions:

1. My purpose for conducting this outreach is to
    *   Build awareness of my library
    *   Introduce a new program, product, or service
    *   Generate qualified leads for future follow-up about a specific service (creating a list of people you want to contact about your new or future programs, products, or services)
    *   Network with customers, community leaders, potential donors, or advocates on a specific topic
    *   Other
2. I want to reach the following audience (include major characteristics of the group, such as sex, age, interest, and income level).
3. I want the following to happen (be specific; for example, I want to get fifty names of people who will want to know about business programs at the library).
4. My key message is: (the piece of information you want your visitors to remember when they leave your table. It should be one sentence and easy to remember; for example, "The library just launched a small business center.")
5. My secondary message:

Plan Your Booth or Table

Now that you know what you want to achieve and whom you want to reach, you need to answer the question, How will I achieve that goal?

I will use the following activities to encourage participation:

Design the Booth

Lay out your booth to indicate the expected path for guests to travel through the area.

Design the Table

Remember, you have only four to six seconds to attract visitors to your booth or table. For a truly attractive look, try to add vertical height to the table rather than have everything at the same level.

What do you want to say?

What message are you communicating?

Say it. Say it. Say it. Say it. Say it. Say it. Say it.

Advocacy

6

It is incredibly easy to set up an advocacy campaign online with Web 2.0 tools. We used WordPress to set up a full blog in two days. The site provides an online headquarters to

1. Set up an online presence (website, wiki, or blog)
2. Determine your call to action
3. Provide supporting materials for taking action
4. Make your case
5. Let other people tell their story about your library
6. Provide an opportunity for supporters to join your cause
7. Set up a social network page
8. Set up a media page

Call to Action

What do you want your supporters to do? Make it simple and say it clearly.

Here are three basic calls to action used for advocacy:

1. Call political leaders (list the phone numbers)
   - Let people know how easy this is to do. Many times people just have to leave their name with a receptionist.
2. Contact your legislator (or council member on the local level)
   - Link to the web page where people can find their representative
   - Include the message you want them to say
3. Sign this petition
   - Use GoPetition; it's a free online petition system
   - Provides space to include an overview of campaign with links to the web page; creates petitions and allows for verification

If you have a budget allotted for your advocacy efforts, Capwiz XC is Capitol Advantage's leading online legislation and advocacy tool that helps organizations send constituent messages to congressional and state legislators. The ALA supports a Capwiz Advocacy Affiliate program for all ALA chapters that want to participate. To learn more about this program, visit www.ala.org.

- Provides a signature list that can be verified and contains comments
- Has social networking capabilities like spreading the word through Tell a Friend; Facebook, Google, and Blogger links; and code to embed in websites

Provide the following supporting materials for taking action—post all documents online with Scribd (www.scribd.com) or another platform that allows people to share:

- Printable flier, bookmark, or postcard with key message
- Printable petition with instructions
- Impact statements
- Legislative agenda
- Phone list of key legislators
- Printable thank-you bookmarks, notes, or postcards

Minnesota, the Southeastern Libraries Cooperating, and the Southeast Library System have created an extraordinary advocacy tool called the Legislative Mashup. The tool maps links to each legislator representing SELCO and SELS libraries with photos and links to legislative pages that list contact e-mail, addresses, and phone numbers at http://tomcat.selco.info/mashups/legislatormashup.html.

Make Your Case

- Provide papers, articles, and other facts that support your cause.
- Publish your documents using an online program, like Scribd, that allows others to easily share them.
- Make it easier for people to share your facts by including a brief summary of each article.

Let Other People Tell Their Stories about Your Library

- Include quotes from people who sign petitions or send letters or e-mail. Print simple quotes with the name separated by a space.

- Include quotes from businesses and organizations that support your library.
- Include stories about people whose lives have been transformed by your library.
- Include videos, photos, and audio files.

Provide an Opportunity for Supporters to Join Your Cause

- Use an online survey service like SurveyMonkey.
- Ask for supporters' names, addresses, e-mail addresses, and comments.
- Follow up with e-mail, online newsletters, or text messages to keep communication flowing.

Sample Text

If you're interested in supporting our cause, please join us. Every member counts. You can help secure the future of libraries in [your community].

Leave us a comment when you sign up. If you don't want your comment published on the website, quoted by the press, or shared for our advocacy efforts, please let us know.

Set Up Social Network Pages

- Set up a Facebook group and invite all your friends and customers to join.
- Set up a LinkedIn group.
- Set up a Flickr group.
- Set up a YouTube channel.
- Provide links back to your website.

Set Up a Media Page

- Post all news releases.
- Include contact information for all spokespeople.

Sample Advocacy Campaigns

A Campaign to Keep a Library Open—Jamesburg Public Library

When Jamesburg Public Library in New Jersey faced a referendum that would
have closed the existing library and created a new sending relationship with
a neighboring library, the Friends group spearheaded a successful advocacy
campaign to vote it down and won. Carole Hetzell, one of the people who
worked on the campaign, claims lawn signs and direct phone calls made the
difference in helping them defeat the referendum.

Source: http://blog.njla.org/

Ohio Libraries

The Ohio Library Council went into full gear when Ohio libraries were faced
with a 50 percent budget cut. They set up an informational page on their
website that outlined the issues, updates on rallies, action steps, and links
that allowed supporters to spread the word with social networks. They set up
a Facebook page and created an image that could be used as a profile picture
by their fans. At the time of this writing, they already had more than 48,000
members join the "Save Ohio Libraries" group.

Source: http://www.olc.org/SaveOhioLibraries.asp

Advocacy Can Change Minds

The public responded to New York Public Library's advocacy campaign "Keep
Your Library Open" by making more than 1,000 donations and sending more
than 30,000 letters and e-mails prompting the city to restore funding to their
libraries.

Source: http://www.nypl.org/

The New Marketing Tools

7

There are so many free Web 2.0 tools available to libraries, from blogs and wikis to sites where you can store and promote your PowerPoint presentations. The trend spotter Helen Blowers, digital strategy director for the Columbus Metropolitan Library in Ohio, created a Web 2.0 learning project called 23 Things (or small exercises), which helps you explore and expand your knowledge of the Internet and Web 2.0. Libraries around the world have replicated the program, which is a great outline for anyone looking to try out new tools.

The most important aspect of any tool is to remember that it should help you achieve a goal. The tools you choose to incorporate in your marketing mix should be the ones that bring the desired results. Ideally, libraries would learn to use the technology and then integrate the appropriate tools into their websites, but that is not always the case for libraries. If we all waited for our IT departments to set up tools for us, most libraries probably wouldn't even have a blog. The library creed for many is, "Build it and your IT department will follow… eventually."

Web 2.0 Tools in a Marketing Mix

Marketing is very simple if you think of your marketing plan as a flowchart for information and view each tool as a communication link on that chart. In the old days any time we tried to reach members, we had to spend a lot of money on printing and mailing. Web 2.0 provides libraries with an affordable way to reach specific audiences with the information that is important to them. The more we understand how those tools work and who uses them, the more effective we are in getting out the message.

Blogging

Many in the library field adopted blogging as a way to get around the red tape and long waits to have things posted on web pages. Those blogs are used as a content management system and seldom allow comments, but they are great for posting photos and videos.

A true blog is a powerful tool that allows libraries to create the two-way conversation that is needed in any WOMM effort. At the very least, it provides an open invitation for members to express their opinions. A successful blog is interesting, relevant to readers, and provides an opportunity for a conversation. It must be kept up to date and on topic.

The question libraries continually struggle with is, Who should be responsible for writing the blog? It depends on how you will be use your blog. If you have a general topic blog about your library, then a team approach probably will work best. Set guidelines for topics and establish style guides for the length of posts, photos, videos, and links. You may want to establish protocols for adding new writers and replacing existing writers to avoid hurt feelings down the road. Ask for volunteers, review the guidelines, and ask that everyone post at least once a month. Even if you have only four volunteers, the blog will be updated every week, which is a good start.

Special Interest Blogs

If you are creating a blog to attract a specific target audience, then you will need writers who have a passion for that subject, because special interest blogs focus on the subject rather than on the library. These have the potential to attract a dedicated network of members to your library. This type of blog is a great companion to a Facebook, or other social networking, account. It requires a high level of participation that can be developed if the library is willing to allow the members a feeling of ownership through program and collection selection.

Wondering what makes a great blog? The Allen County Public Library blog is so mind blowing that we jotted down notes on the back of a bookmark. Here they are:

Love the plain language they use: "On our blog—acpl.info—we'll post cool websites, highlight materials available at the library, and share information about library services you may not have heard of before. You're welcome to add your two cents, ask questions, make comments, and generally take part in the conversation. We want to hear from you!"

What makes this blog stand out is that the writers (twenty-eight of them) have written short posts that reflect their intelligence, wit, charm, curiosity, and storytelling abilities to put together a "blogversation" of the highest quality. How refreshing to see a blog that actually encourages interactivity. They blend in short updates of the library's news and events.

I loved the humorous blogversation about how their librarians were beginning to look alike. The links to Flickr pictures of staff members dressing in the same colors and wearing similar hairstyles were hysterical. Simple postings like the one lamenting the passing of an author with links to his books were great marketing strategies.

Adding a book display in the library is the icing on the cake. The other post that caught my attention was about the author's chance meeting of a local celebrity. I loved it because it was personal and helped the reader continue to create his experience.

Are Young Adult Blogs Special Interest Blogs?

Blogs for young adults are not really special interest blogs, but there are special interests within the YA category that you can tap into. Even gaming can be divided into smaller groups according to popular games. But keep in mind that your blog has to have a different approach than other blogs, or you'll be competing rather than meeting needs.

Seven Simple Ways for Libraries to Promote a Blog

1. Add the link to your e-mail signature.
2. Add the link to your business card.
3. Create links on different pages throughout the website.
4. Put the blog on the front page of the library's website.
5. Begin a conversation at someone else's blog and leave a comment, which will link back to your blog.
6. Leave comments about news articles that relate to your blog. It's best to try to be in the top ten. It's too easy to get lost when there are pages of comments.
7. Cross-market with your social media sites.

To Allow or Not to Allow Comments

It's amazing how many libraries didn't want to allow comments because they were afraid that it might give complainers a public podium. You'd think the library would welcome open debate. A speaker once mentioned that when a negative comment was posted on a blog, other comments stood up to the dissenter.

Guidelines:

1. Set clear guidelines for what will and will not be tolerated. Be sure to include that posts may not include names of other people or personal accusations. You don't have to reinvent the wheel—look at other sites. Yahoo! Buzz has a few dos and don'ts that make sense.
2. Do not allow anonymous posts.
3. Approve comments before posting. Eliminate only those that don't meet the guidelines.
4. When a complaint is posted, respond. This is a forum, and if looked at from a positive perspective, it can offer libraries the chance to debate, advocate, and elucidate.

5. Reserve the right to refuse or remove any comments that do not comply with your guidelines.

There are a lot of blogs by librarians for librarians, and some blogs by librarians for the public, but how are we doing with blogs by the public for the public about libraries?

Blogs are a great medium for WOMM, so why not make an effort to build some relationships to spread the word about your library? One way to start the conversation is to search out blogs by your customers and leave a comment. Go the step beyond and write about them in your blogs or, at the very least, include links to their blogs. If you develop a blog with a clear purpose that stays on point, it can position you and your library as a reliable place to find information.

Should You Be Blogging?

A friend of ours is a director for a small public library. One day Nancy got into a conversation about blogs: "I was telling her how excited I was about writing my blog and how it was helping me connect my ideas to libraries around the world. She just looked at me and said, 'When in the world do you write this thing?'"

"'Well, I write it at different times, 2 a.m. when I can't sleep, 6 a.m. when I'm reading the newspaper, Saturday mornings…'"

"She interrupted: 'Wait a minute, stop right there… I am not interested in one more thing that I have to add to my plate, especially something that will require me to write in the few moments of personal time I have left in my life. Two o'clock in the morning? Are you crazy?'"

She had a good point and it got Nancy thinking about blogging and how it can fit into the already overcrowded schedules of all of us.

When Jenny Levine brought blogging to the library world in 1995 with her *Librarian du jour* blog, most of us were still struggling to learn how to cut and paste in a Word document. Levine's quick daily updates not only shared information but also began to create what has evolved into social networking—though back then it might have been considered letter writing on steroids. Since then thousands of library blogs have been created, but the question still remains, Are they worth the time spent writing them?

The answer is yes—and no. Yes, if it helps your organization fulfill its mission and goals. No, if it doesn't. Yes, if it can add value to your reader's life. No, if it can't.

Now that's not to say that your staff can't create blogs on other subjects and write them on their own time, but if you are going to have staff write a blog on company time, then it only makes sense to have the content be connected to your mission or goals and to make sure it can add value to those who read it. We're betting the chances are high that blogging will make sense for your library.

Are You a Web 2.0 Librarian Living in a 1.0 Library? Don't Fret—It's Easy and Fun to Bring Anyone Up to Date

What Is a Blog Anyway?

A blog is a log of entries posted on a website. Originally called weblogs, the name was shortened to *blog*. The postings are displayed in reverse chronological order and can provide commentaries or news about various topics. Blog postings consist of text often accompanied by images or video and links that readers can follow for additional information.

Other Kinds of Blogs

Not a writer? Why not consider using another medium to communicate?

Vlogs are just like blogs only instead of using text, the vlogger uses video. And those who prefer speaking to writing may be interested in creating podcasts.

The World of Blogging

Welcome to the world of blogs. All the blogs in the universe live in a place called the blogosphere. It's not an actual place that can be found on a geography map, but this virtual world has more than 100 million blogs in is community, and the number is growing every day. Each blog is located at a blog site. If you write a blog, you will have earned the title of blogger. If you add a list of blogs with links to those pages, then you will have created a blog roll on your blog.

Need to Convince Yourself to Start a Blog?

Here are three good reasons to start a blog:

1. They are free, easy to use, and immediate. The programs that you can use to create a blog such as Blogger (www.blogger.com) are free. You can set up and publish a new blog in less than five minutes.

2. A blog is a great communication tool to keep your customers up to date on news about your organization. It is easy to add photos and even videos, so blogs can have a great visual appeal for readers.
3. Blogs offer great measurements.

Here are three ways to convince your boss to let you start a blog:

1. Connect the dots. Read your library's strategic plan, mission statement, department goals, personal goals, and the like, to find the goals that will be met through the development of a blog. Write out the purpose of your blog linked to those goals.
2. Show the feasibility. The major problems facing libraries are often time and money. If that is the case, explain how you can develop the blog on free software and link to it from the present website. Be sure to keep your explanation simple. Outline who the contributors will be and how much staff time will be allotted for updating.
3. Present it as a pilot project. If you are still encountering resistance, suggest that you blog for six months and evaluate it at that point.

Secrets to a Successful Blog

If you are thinking about creating a new blog, here are some quick tips:

Create a Specific Topic for the Blog and Keep All Posts to That Theme

The M Word was created to explore marketing ideas for libraries. Later Nancy became more interested in videos about libraries. When she saw that there wasn't a blog on that topic she decided to create a new blog rather than dilute her message. Other people have created blogs that have a more general focus to give them leeway to include various topics that all relate to one theme, such as libraries. An excellent example is *The Library Garden*. Six librarians with different perspectives (public, academic, school, consortia, youth) share the goal of ensuring the health and relevance of libraries. The mix works well, and there are enough people involved to keep content interesting without being overly time consuming for any one individual.

Keep Your Postings Short

The shorter, the better. No one has a lot of time to read long posts.

Break It Up

If you have a great post but it's too long, break it into segments and post one each day. Let readers know that you'll be writing more the next day.

Keep It Business Personal

Business personal is just like business casual. Its OK to dress down on casual Friday, but no one expects you to show up in those comfy sweatpants you like to wear around the house. Blogs have the same boundaries. They should definitely have a personal voice and reflect your personality, but the content should never contain gossip or delve into personal problems.

Loosen Up

There's been a huge debate in the blogosphere about whether blogs should have the same standards of other print media. The debate has gone as far as questioning whether it even matters whether bloggers need to worry about spelling. The debate exists because the whole idea of blogging is that it is immediate, and with that comes the possibility of typos. As more and more blogs begin to represent businesses, there needs to be a middle ground that will allow spontaneity while upholding basic standards. So hold your ground on spelling and grammar, but loosen up when it comes to phrasing. No one expects to find great literature on a blog; they are looking for information on a continuing basis and are willing to leave well-turned phrasing to print media.

Be Open to Controversy

Readers like to read controversial points of view. We don't advise that you write to stir emotions for the sake of stirring emotions, but don't be afraid to offer up thoughts that might not find universal agreement with everyone. Those posts are often the ones most read and shared.

Include Tools for Readers to Share Your Posts

Make sure your readers can subscribe to your blog. Also provide tools for them to share the posts with friends through e-mail and social networks. A popular tool is ShareThis, but there are others, and new tools are being developed every day.

Avoid Blogout

It happens to us all. We put our energy into creating a blog and have gotten pretty consistent at posting. Readership is up and ideas are plentiful and free flowing. Then you get a new responsibility at work, join a new committee, or spend a little extra time with the family. Before you know it, you're past the great tipping point, and there you are at two in the morning barely getting through a post before you fall asleep at your computer. As you look in the mirror and see the imprint of your keyboard in your face, you realize that you have blogout, the bloggers' equivalent of burnout. Before you delete that blog, take a minute to think about another possibility.

Enlist New Writers for Your Blog

Sure, it started as your baby, but don't think of this as giving up custody—consider it calling in the village to raise the child. If you are writing for a universal audience, why not enlist a few other people in your field to join you? Don't ask fellow bloggers, because chances are that they have their own version of blogout. Between the Web and your own business connections in committees or groups, you have a wealth of choices. Don't offer a full partnership; just ask whether they'd like to be a guest writer and see how they do. It is always better to be in the position to ask someone to post more than to have to ask them to post less. If you are writing a blog about your library, why not consider having local residents come in as guest bloggers? Take a few minutes to teach them how to post directly and see how it works out. When Michael Stephens (*Tame the Web*) was finishing up his doctoral dissertation, he had several people write guest columns. It not only was interesting for the readers but also gave the bloggers a new audience.

Increasing Traffic to Your Blog

+ Leaving a comment on someone else's blog is one of the best ways to increase traffic to your blog. Look for blogs that relate to your blog's topic. If it's a blog that normally gets lots of comments, try to be one of the first people to comment and make sure you mention your blog!
+ Mention your blog at events and list the address on your fliers, newsletters, and e-mail.
+ Include posts on your Facebook and MySpace pages.

- Link to other blogs that you enjoy reading. This is a way for your readers to know what interests you, but the blogs you link to will be more willing to link back to your site.

- Add the blog to your business cards. Better yet, create business cards just for your blog. Get creative and copy the MOO card idea by making miniature cards with cool photos from your blog on them.

- Add your reviews at Amazon.com. If your blog has reviews of books, be sure to also post them to Amazon.com. Amazon offers readers the neat feature of clicking on the reviewer's name to see everything they've written.

The Next Step: Making a New Marketing Mix around Web 2.0

As we move along the Web 2.0 continuum, new software has become available that allows for exciting web design, such as user-generated content created by both staff and library customers, which results in interactive sites. One day we will view blogs in the same way that this generation of gamers views the 1970s video game Pong.

We've been seeing a lot of buzz about the traditional marketing mix of the four *P*s (place, price, promotion, and product) changing to fit the new Web 2.0 world by adding two more *P*s: people and process. Robert Lauterborn came up with the four *C*s: convenience, cost to the user, communication, and customer needs and wants.

Don't get bogged down with the terminology. Create a marketing mix that offers a great product, develop a communication network that allows for communication about the product, and provide opportunities for open conversations between your library and customers.

Don't worry about all the technology out there. Start with basics.

Create a website and blog. Some libraries are even using blogs instead of a website. Remember that when it comes to marketing, content is king, so you need to have an online presence that continually offers new information.

Sign up for a social network account. If your customers use Facebook, go with Facebook. Don't try to be the leader and convince people to use your network. When it comes to social networks, it is always best to follow the crowd when it comes to marketing, so join the ones most popular with your customers.

Create a social media plan. Your plan should include posting videos to YouTube and photos to Flickr. Make sure you create groups where your users can post their creations.

Create a communication network. Electronic mailing lists and online newsletters are still the easiest and least expensive way to e-mail messages to target audiences. But new trends like Twitter are always emerging. Watch for the ways your target audience communicates and follow along. The hottest trend now is mobile phone marketing. The start-up costs are still high, but with increasing use of mobile phones, this is sure to become the best way to communicate with your customers.

Advertising

You probably don't have a large budget for advertising. Google offers a grant program for 501(c)(3) organizations that provides a free AdWords campaign. With AdWords, your library appears in the Sponsored Links section when people conduct a Google search with related keywords. Even if you can't qualify for the grant, AdWords are an affordable way to reach targeted online users. You can predetermine your budget and pay only for people who click on your link. Google even provides measurement tools. This program is well worth investigating for your library.

With new media, the idea of putting money into any type of newspaper or magazine advertising may not be the best use of your budget. The exception to this might be long-term collaborative ads where you partner with other companies for a well-branded, highly visible ad campaign. A better use of your money might be to invest in creating a well-designed ad campaign that lends itself to print materials, banner ads on your website, and widgets for your social networks. If you are creating WOMM campaigns, you can use advertising dollars much more effectively to create exciting messages and visuals.

Google Business Center

An invaluable resource for your library is the Google Business Center. If your library isn't listed, it should be! Not only will your library's information appear when searched, as an added bonus Google will allow you to add coupons to your Google Maps Listing—free! You could offer discounts for printing, faxing, or copying services at your library or offer coupons for the library store, paid programs, or give a free book sale item. Partner with a local business. The ideas are limitless.

PowerPoint Presentations

Every time you give a presentation, you are marketing your library and its services. You put a lot of work into creating a PowerPoint presentation. One way to extend the reach of your presentation is to allow others to use it for their presentations. Offer it to community groups and local businesses. This is a great way to help other groups get out the word about your library. Another way is to post the presentation to a social networking site, such as SlideShare, to let people view it directly. Another option is to create a short presentation to embed in your news releases. Be sure to use lots of interesting photos, informative charts, and short sentences.

Twitter aspires to be something different from social-networking sites like Facebook or MySpace: rather than being a vast self-contained world centered on one website, Twitter dreams of being a tool that people can use to communicate with each other from a multitude of locations, like e-mail. You do not have to visit the home site to send a message, or tweet. Tweets can originate from text-messaging on a cellphone or even blogging software. Likewise, tweets can be read remotely, whether as text messages or, say, "status updates" on a friend's Facebook page.

—Noam Cohen

Source: New York Times *online edition, June 20, 2009*

Twitter

When we first began writing this book, Twitter was just gaining popularity. It has quickly become a major new trend and a terrific marketing tool. It is a service that allows you to update your status with short messages (up to 140 characters), just like an SMS text message. What makes it special are the social elements that allow users to follow one another. Whenever you're following somebody on Twitter, you are able to instantly receive their updates and keep up to date with their status. By adding elements of mobility and speed, Twitter allows you to update your status via the web page, instant messaging, mobile phone, BlackBerry, or various other third-party applications.

An incredible example of the power of "tweeting" occurred in, of all places, Topeka, Kansas, home of David Lee King (www.davidleeking.com). David's library, the Topeka and Shawnee County Public Library, had a board meeting to vote on restricting access to four books in the collection. David and the general manager of the local TV station were tweeting the public comments and deliberations of the board. Because David also posted his "tweets" to his Facebook account, quite a few librarians and community members were following him. At one point, their hashtag (a Twitter tag that's added to your post) was the seventh-hottest trend on Twitter that evening.

Twitter is quickly turning the desire for real-time information into a need for minute-by-minute updates. There is no doubt that there will be more advances in technology that will one day make Twitter seem too slow. As marketers, our job is to be aware of the tools as they emerge and to choose those that help us best communicate our message.

Twitter is one trend you probably won't want to ignore. The ways you can market with Twitter are endless. Trends like these have the potential to change marketing paradigms. Here are some suggestions on how you can use Twitter to market your library:

- Tweet about new materials.
- Tweet about legislative issues that affect your library.
- Tweet top links for popular topics.
- Tweet "Best Reference Questions."
- Rebroadcast local news.
- Tweet during programs—include pictures!
- Tweet "Quotes for the Day."
- Tweet interesting facts.
- Tweet during conferences.
- Tweet interesting comments that you overhear from customers.

Wikis

When it comes to marketing with a wiki, a great place to start is posting your library's information on Wikipedia. Take the time to add content from your collections with links back to your library. You can also create your own wiki as a way to collaborate with your community to build content for programs. Wikis are excellent vehicles to engage organizations and businesses to share their expertise on various topics and link to the resource from their own pages.

LinkedIn

A social network site for professionals, LinkedIn helps you connect with other professionals and the business audience. You can create groups along the same concept as Facebook.

Mobile Phones

Popular television shows like *American Idol* have engaged people to text their vote, and political campaigns have asked people to sign up for news alerts—this has helped make mobile marketing the emergent advertising method in the United States. Mobile marketing is already popular outside of the United States, and as consumer confidence grows and technology like videos becomes commonplace on mobile phones, mobile marketing is sure to be an important tool for librarians.

Library customers use mobile phones. Texting is a common practice, and photo sharing is catching on quickly as well. It only makes sense for libraries to begin to take advantage of this new technology to reach target audiences as part of a communication network.

Some possible uses for mobile marketing are the following:

+ Contests
+ Voting
+ Retrieving files like free ring tones
+ Event updates
+ Product or service information
+ On-demand updates (information about specific topics)
+ Opting in to receive videos

Flickr

Between inexpensive digital cameras and mobile phones, every moment in our lives is now a Kodak moment. Posting your photos to a social networking site like Flickr is an easy way to allow others to view and share photos from your library. You can choose the level of Creative Commons licensing you want for each photo, group them into sets and categories, tag them, and automatically post them to your blog. You can even create groups so that your customers can add their photos. You should have a lawyer-approved photo policy in place for your library before posting photos. Once that's in place, you are good to go.

Tagging

Libraries around the world have already tapped into tagging tools with great success. The Library of Congress launched its The Commons pilot program, which invited the public to tag and describe two sets of approximately three thousand historical photos. According to the Library of Congress's website (www.flickr.com/photos/library_of_congress/), those photos average approximately 500,000 views a month and have surpassed the 10 million mark in total views.

Libraries can apply this concept for other marketing efforts as well by encouraging customers to tag any photos they post to Flickr.

Ways to Get Your Flickr Movement Going

+ Create a group.
+ Encourage community members to tag their photos with your library's group name.
+ Post signs in your library asking people who post photos of your library to tag them with a tag of your choosing.

Ideas for Using Flickr in Your Library

+ Give a virtual tour of your library.
+ Start a Flickr group for your YA group, friends, or interest groups.
+ Tell the history of your library in pictures.
+ Find Flickr groups of interest to your community and promote the groups or specific images.
+ Partner with local museums, community groups, and schools to create an online collection of photos around a specific topic.
+ Show pictures of regular community meetings held at your library.

Examples of Photos to Post

+ Library, campus, and community events
+ Author visits, gaming tournaments, and festivals
+ Images of rare collections
+ New items in your library

- Customers, volunteers, friends, and trustees
- Selected public domain photos from databases
- Conferences, workshops, and classes

Photo Permission

Whenever the subject of photos comes up, questions about permission are sure to follow. Check with your lawyer to ensure that your forms are aligned with your state's laws. The rule of thumb for libraries is to have permission forms signed. Parents and guardians need to sign permission forms for children younger than eighteen. Make sure the form mentions that all videos and photos are the property of your library and may be used in print.

Quick Tips for Getting Permission Slips Signed

Include a paragraph on all registration forms and have adults and parents sign it as part of the form. Include a place for parents to opt out and require that they include contact information so that you can reach them if needed. Make sure that people who do not want their photo taken are out of range of any pictures you'll be taking.

For adult programs, make up a permission form with lots of spaces for signatures and names, put it on a clipboard, and pass it around. Be sure to announce what you are doing and let them know that they should tell you if they don't want their picture taken.

Videos

Videos have an unlimited potential for marketing your library. It is free to post them to the Web, where they can remain indefinitely. They are easily embedded into you're your web pages, blogs, and Facebook and MySpace pages. Even if you don't have the budget to purchase equipment or the staff to create them, there are plenty of people in your community who would be more than willing to make them for you—for free.

Before you send out a call for videos, though, it's a good idea to ask yourself what you want the videos to do for your library. Here are a few basic categories:

- Awareness of ongoing programs, products, or services that your library offers
- The "cool" factor for teens
- Visual networking connection for groups in your community

- Promotion of specific library-sponsored programs, products, and services
- PSAs
- Commercials
- Advocacy

Questions to Answer When Making a Video

- What do you want to say?
- Who will be your audience?
- How and where will the video be shown?

The price is right, but video marketing in the age of YouTube is more than creating a commercial. It is a way to get your customers to participate in telling your library's story. The trouble with videos is that they can be time consuming to make and edit. The good news is that you don't have to make them. If you don't have the staff or budget, you can enlist your customers to create videos for you, have them post them to YouTube, and then just cut and paste the embedding code to your web page, blogs, and MySpace pages. You can also include the link in your newsletters and as part of your e-mail signature. In other words, let others create the video and just join in to get the word out.

Funny, Cool, or Inappropriate?

Cool videos are short, often silly, and seldom focused on one topic. They feature tweens and teens being themselves and having fun in the library. Many libraries have institutionalized this type of video by turning them into projects. That works, but the authentic cool video can be as simple as kids running in the library, laughing at one another, and spitting water out of their noses—or even the ten-second gotcha shot. Although these may not be appropriate for the front page of your website, they fit perfectly on your MySpace pages and are great for MySpace friends to post to their pages. Be careful, though, that there is no ridicule or meanness on the part of the kids. The ultimate cool-factor cult video, *Silent Library*, with special guest Ernesto Hoost, has more than a million views. It is actually a clip from the Japanese variety show *Gaki no tsukai ya arahende* and combines teen humor with survival torture tricks. The video of a simple game in which the loser suffers various pranks while keeping his or her laughter to a library quiet has attracted fans throughout the world. While immensely popular, it's likely inappropriate for your library. While librarians like to star in funny movies, they often are funnier for librarians than for teens. A rule of thumb is that teens acting weird are funny, but librarians acting funny are weird.

Where to Upload Your Videos

There are plenty of great platforms for uploading your videos. YouTube is one, but other video-sharing sites include Google Video, Yahoo! Video, blip .tv, and Kaltura. The advantage of YouTube is that it is the number one site, so you can easily embed YouTube videos on most social networking pages, which is important for beginners. You can keep your eyes open for other sites, and you may even decide that others have better quality. Beginners, though, should keep it simple and use YouTube.

YouTube

+ YouTube shows more than 100 million videos per day.
+ Videos cannot exceed ten minutes in length, unless you have a director's account. But even with a director's account, you don't want to post videos longer than ten minutes. We encourage you to keep them under thirty seconds, at least in the beginning.
+ Before uploading your organization's video, select a category such as News, and then tag it with keywords for viewers to find it easily. If you fill out all the information about your video, it will get better reach with search engines.
+ You can allow any YouTube visitor to cut and paste HTML code that will embed your video in his or her own website or blog.
+ YouTube lets you create playlists of your favorite videos and even build your own custom channel, which is useful if your organization wants to highlight clips related to its cause or those of similar nonprofits.

I love public radio and television, but it's time for them to become two-way media.

Next time we go to war, and we seem to be doing that all too regularly, we must be certain that the kinds of conversations that ordinary people have about the motives of our political leaders make it onto the airwaves.

And I'd like to know what the pundits are saying when they go out to dinner, not just when they're on the air. We knew Bush was lying in the lead-up to the war, now let's reform the media so those thoughts get proper coverage in time to avoid national catastrophes like the war in Iraq.

—David Winer, *first podcast, July 20, 2003*

Facebook

There has been some discussion about a dilemma that kids on Facebook have: their parents wanting to be their "friends." That got us wondering about how effective our libraries have been in engaging interactive online conversations with teens. We have been working so hard to reach teens. Libraries have blogs, Facebook accounts, and MySpace pages, but are we really able to be part of kids' interactive network or are we still pushing—trying a little too hard, like the kid who just isn't part of the group?

Are we using the tools that will help us make that connection, or are we re-creating a classroom setting and labeling it "new"?

We found a great video featuring a teen talking about Wii and the teen group and we loved it. It is a very cool video with a teen speaking to teens, the whole bit. But it had only 228 hits. When the hits are that low for an online video designed to reach teens, to me that's a red flag that says we missed the mark. Let's face it, even a very cool teen talking about a teen center just doesn't cut it. We might want to use these tools a little differently.

All the new marketing concepts are about providing what our customers want. So what do our teens want? We don't think kids necessarily need us to be their friends in the classic sense. Hey—like it or not, we are still adults. We may be cooler than a classroom, but we are an institution. With those parameters, what kind of social networking do teens need from us?

Let's start where we are successful. If we run programs that bring in teens and they leave thinking it was an awesome program, then we can assume they'll want to tell their friends who didn't come what they missed and share memories with those who did come. This is where posting a YouTube clip would help. There's no need to make a video of the whole event, but you could edit the memorable clips, and kids on YouTube will view them. Chances are extremely good that you'll need a teen in the editing room with you to pick them out or else you'll miss what they really thought was good. You might follow through with a link to an online survey about either the program or the clips—something that will bring them to the teen blog where they can find out and vote for the next program.

Speaking of blogs, how are your teen group blogs doing? Is anyone running them as a place where teens voice opinions on issues they are already thinking about and maybe even discussing?

We all love online book clubs, and there is an audience for them. But we also know that teens love to talk about themselves. They like to talk about the things they are reading in teen magazines—older brothers harassing them, too-hard homework, adults acting like hypocrites, prom, celebrity gossip, and the like. Is there a way we can use the topics they are interested in to engage them in an online conversation with us?

You probably need to start with online surveys to build some interest because surveys allow kids to be involved with the safety of anonymity. If an issue is getting enough traction, then maybe open it up to online discussions.

YouTube debates are a big hit. Why not use the medium for your teens? Attach secondary polls asking kids to name people they'd like to question about the topic. Or take it a step further and ask them what famous people they would want to question. This starts the list of people you'll want to try to contact. You don't have to bring the person to your library; you could negotiate an online appearance and perhaps run a webinar. Teens can submit YouTube questions and vote for which ones to ask the person. You might be able to land a really big name if you join with other libraries and schools and split costs. And the beauty is that because it's online you'll be able to reach kids at home.

Podcasting

Podcasting—The Next Wave

Libraries are just entering the world of podcasting. From a marketing point of view, the idea of having people download a forty-five-minute presentation from your library and plug it into their ears while tuning out the rest of the world is about as good as it gets. The trouble is that unless you do it well, no one will want to plug you in more than once.

It's All about You

More than 20 million people listen to podcasts—who will be listening to yours?

People listen to podcasts because they are passionate about a subject. They want to hear from people who are as passionate.

Start by asking yourself

- What's unique about you?
- Who are your listeners?
- Who are you to your listeners?

Content Is Everything

Stay away from lectures; people want to listen to engaging personalities. If you think about it, the very act of placing an earbud into your ear and turning on the iPod is about as intimate as you can get with a person. People do not want hours of your library or a list of upcoming events whispered in their ears. If you keep in mind that podcasts are about building relationships, you will be able to keep focused.

Questions to answer:

+ What do you want to accomplish?
+ How many people do you want to reach?
+ What is your competition?

Will They Listen?

There are plenty of topics that make for an interesting podcast from your library. Think of what you are doing that people are passionate about. Here are some ideas:

+ The series—pick a topic and run a series; *Adventures of Gastronomy* took people from the farm to production to bars detailing the story about tequila
+ Commentary, documentary, infomercial
+ Distilling information—taking lots of information into daily or weekly podcasts
+ Case studies
+ Holistic programming—podcast author, include precasts about upcoming programming and links to resources
+ Metadata—top-ten lists
+ Magazine style—tour the area, interesting stops, people, and so on
+ Offer help—how to podcast
+ Grow—look at other fields and what they are doing
+ Find people with great ideas and promote those ideas
+ Produce audiobooks
+ Think beyond your own show and be a guest

Important tip: Be consistent and engaged. You don't have to give a show once a week, but whatever the timing is, keep it consistent.

To Edit or Not to Edit

Forget about going live. Be kind to your listeners and edit. There is a certain appeal for some live shows, but unless you have conquered dead space, ums, and clucking tongues, your podcast will sound much better if you edit it.

This will add a lot of time to your schedule, but it is better to produce one outstanding show a month than to create fours shows that no one wants to listen to.

A general rule of thumb is to schedule ten minutes for every minute for each of your podcasts.

Marketing Your Podcast

+ Include show notes or the outline of your show.
+ Consider having exceptional podcasts in whole or portions transcribed and posted to your blog.
+ Remember to use keywords.
+ Feel free to use jargon for microcommunities.
+ Fill out podcast information—name, artist, album, and so on.
+ The lyric tag will show up in iPhone (four thousand characters).
+ For file names, use hyphens between show name, date, and episode number.
+ Provide RSS feeds and iTunes subscriptions.
+ Announce future shows.

Preproduction

Soundproof your environment to the best of your ability. The cleaner you can make the recording, the easier it will be to get great sound.

Clear the room of sound busters. Turn off the cell phone, air-conditioning, and fans. If you are recording at home, turn off any household appliances. Be cognizant of outside noises such as airplanes, loud traffic, and cars with loud stereos blasting. Night is a great time to record.

Help your sound behave. Seal the noise in your room by plugging the bottom of the door and close the windows. If your computer's fan is loud, consider putting the computer in a closet during the recording.

Tame the good sound. There are two ways to break up sound: absorption and diffusion. Soft items like foam pads on the walls help absorb sound. Anything with texture helps absorb sound. You could put items like blankets or egg-crate mattress pads on the walls. The idea behind diffusing sound is to break up flat surfaces. You can buy panels designed to scatter the sound, or you can make some by breaking up flat surfaces yourself. If you have a bookshelf, consider regrouping the books with different sizes and depths. Cover the floor with a rug.

The Microphone

Buy what you can afford but buy the right microphone.

Directional Properties

Every microphone has a property known as directionality, which is the microphone's sensitivity to sound from various directions.

- **Omnidirectional** microphones pick up sound equally from all directions. Because such microphones pile up all sound equally, these are not the best microphones for podcasting.
- **Unidirectional** microphones pick up sound from only one direction.
- **Cardioid** means "heart-shaped," which is the type of pickup pattern such mics use. They pick up sound mostly from the front and from the sides to a lesser extent. Cardioid mics emphasize sound from the direction the mic is pointed, which gives some leeway for mic movement and ambient noise. Handheld mics are usually cardioid.
- **Hypercardioid** is a variation of the cardioid microphone. It is very directional and eliminates most sound from the sides and rear. Because of the long, thin design of hypercardioids, they are often referred to as shotgun microphones. These are great mics to use when there is a lot of ambient noise, because they isolate the sound, but you have to be careful to keep the mic pointed at the subject or you'll lose the audio.
- **Bidirectional** microphones use a figure-eight pattern and pick up sound equally from two opposite directions. This is a great microphone for an interview with two people facing each other (with the microphone between them).

If you want to learn more about microphones, see the great article "How Microphones Work" at Media College (www.mediacollege.com/audio/microphones/how-microphones-work.html).

How Much Is Enough?

You do not need to spend a fortune to make a great podcast. The Blue Snowball microphone sells for less than $100 and is a popular choice of many podcasters. It connects to your computer via USB and is self-powered, so you don't need to worry about external power supplies. It has a unique three-pattern switch (unidirectional and omnidirectional) that gives you everything you need for podcasting and recording your own rock music!

Blue just introduced a smaller cardioid travel mic called the Snowflake that is designed to allow you to place it on a desk or flat surface near your computer, or mount it to the screen of most laptops. It costs about $70.

Rode is a company in Australia that makes incredible handmade microphones. They have come out with the Podcaster mic in the $225 price range that has gotten great reviews. It connects to your computer via USB and is self-powered. The mic ships with a USB cable and a mic stand adapter, so it's ready to go when you take it out of the box. No special drivers are needed, either.

Shure produces great mics as well. The SM58 is known to be the workhorse of the industry. It isn't a USB mic, so it does need a cable.

Mic Tips

If you are using a unidirectional mic, think of it as a laser and be sure to point it at your mouth. To determine how close and the exact location conduct a grid test. Record your voice in each location and then play it back and decide on the best placement for your speaking style.

If your *P*s are popping, use a pop filter or screen, which is available for $15. If you need one in an emergency, tie nylons with a rubber band to a wire hanger. You can also move slightly to the left or right of the mic. If you're using a unidirectional mic, if the popping is too great, you can point the microphone at neck level.

Adjust the height of your mic with a gooseneck attachment, which allows you to turn the mic for interviews.

Purchase a windscreen to block wind during outdoor recording.

You can use adapters to turn your mic into a USB mic. The MXL Mic Mate (about $50) has a product test on YouTube (tinyurl.com/mic-mate-vid).

With lateral movements, when you are positioned directly in front of the microphone (or on axis), it is crucial that you remain in this orientation to ensure a consistent tone. Moving to either side of the microphone will create drastic tonal changes—making your voice sound muffled, as without treble (clarity), which is known as being off axis from the microphone.

With proximate movements, moving closer to and farther away from the microphone creates drastic volume (amplitude) changes. It is essential that you remain the same distance from the microphone to ensure a consistent volume.

Proximity effect is when you move closer to a directional microphone, the kind most engineers use, your voice will be fuller, richer, and have more bass (less treble).

When a full-bodied, sexy, or deep tone is required, use proximity effect to your advantage—stand about three to four inches from the mic. When you desire a thinner sound, try standing six to eight inches away.

Voice Tips

+ It's all in the breath—breathe!
+ Stand or sit up straight so that your sternum and the small of your back are straight.
+ Speak to the back of room.
+ Don't shout.
+ Speak naturally.
+ Smile when you speak.

On the Road

If you are at a conference, look for smaller areas; for example, a breakout room will give you better sound than a large convention hall. Consider recording in your car—minivans have been known to serve as recording studios.

Digital Recording

A good digital recorder allows you to capture great audio quality when you are on the road. The Zoom H2 from Samson is everything you'll need with a price tag of less than $150. It's a portable recorder with four microphone capsules that offer you the option of recording from the front, back, or both sides of the recorder. This allows you the flexibility to record speakers at a conference, to include audience comments, and even to conduct interviews. The new H4 has more bells and whistles and costs about $100 more.

Olympus introduced its newest line of PCM recorders with the launch of the LC-10, which allows you to record audio and play back the files in three recording formats: WAV, MP3, and WMA. The price tag runs at about $300 to $400.

Grid Test

Record yourself in front of the microphone in each of the following locations. Play the audio back to determine the best mic position for your voice.

Left Top
2 inches
3 inches
4 inches
5 inches
6 inches

Right Top
2 inches
3 inches
4 inches
5 inches
6 inches

Center
2 inches
3 inches
4 inches
5 inches
6 inches

Left Bottom
2 inches
3 inches
4 inches
5 inches
6 inches

Right Bottom
2 inches
3 inches
4 inches
5 inches
6 inches

Tips for Making a Great Podcast

- Plan your podcast.
- First rehearse, then record.
- Be concise and don't be overambitious: concentrate on the key points you want to get across and don't lose focus.
- Mash up with other podcasts using Creative Commons licenses.
- Use a music sound track.
- Make sure you've centered the tracks and balanced volume levels.
- After you've edited the piece, take a break and then listen one more time.
- Organize it by adding chapters so your listeners can to go back and listen to one part without having to listen to the whole podcast again.
- Make sure you add show notes as well.
- Add artwork to your chapters. That way your listeners will have a visual accompaniment to what they are listening to.
- Once you have chapters, you can also add links to the chapters so listeners can click on a URL for more information.
- In addition to factual information, you can also add advisory information for your podcast—anything from clean (appropriate for all ages) to explicit.

Writing a Script

1. Start with a theme and make a list of ideas that connect to that theme.
2. Ask yourself what your audience would want to hear.
3. Create an outline of bullet points.
4. If you are interviewing someone, create a green sheet with your written introduction, three to five questions, biographical information in bullet points, and a bibliography of sources.
5. Read through the script with another person to get feedback or record your show and play it back.
6. Create the podcast.

Interviews

Preinterview

- Create a green sheet.
- Research personal information and know about what the person is best known for and important dates.
- You can share the focus of the interview but avoid sending the actual questions. The answers often sound too rehearsed, which brings down the energy of the interview.

Tips for Recording the Interview

- Use Skype (they have a service that allows you to call any cell or landline for about $30 a year).
- Use Call Recorder to record the conversation. The site has great tools that allow you to change the audio into separate tracks and convert it into MP3 files.

Design

Dollar-Store Solutions

Dollar-store solutions are tips that you can use to create professional-quality results with a penny-pinching boss looking over your shoulder.

- Banish clip art with istockphoto.com, affordable and high-quality stock photos and illustrations.
- Students in local design programs are always looking for projects to fill out their portfolios. Give them an opportunity to do some creative work for you, and it's a win-win situation.
- Use http://gimp.org, a free open-source alternative to Photoshop.
- The Library of Congress Prints and Photographs collection (www.loc.gov) is a great place to find super-high-resolution images or to browse for ideas.
- Browse around stock photo subscription sites like photos.com or shutterstock.com. If you like the selection, consider joining if you plan on using thirty or more stock images in a year.
- Library archives offer a veritable treasure trove of images for the picking.
- Browse marketing blogs for inspiration (see bitesizedmarketing.com for a list of sites).
- See http://adsoftheworld.com for a wonderful collection of successful advertisements and marketing campaigns from around the world.
- Online print companies are a great way to get small full-color print jobs produced for very little money. Check out www.jakprints.com.
- Most new higher-end color printers can print on 11-inch-by-17-inch paper, which is a great size for producing in-house posters easily and cheaply.
- Search www.zoo-m.com/flickr-storm/ to use Creative Commons photos from Flickr.
- Does anyone on your staff have any formal design training? See if they would like to design your promotional materials.
- Ganged printers are a cheap and effective way to produce some of your print materials, like postcard invitations for events. (See ganged printers, page 117.)

You and Your New Best Friend (Hint, It's a Designer)

Initial Stage of Working with a Designer

Designers are notoriously hard to work with. Here are a few tips to make your interaction with them more beneficial for the both of you.

The reason that designers are so hard to work with is that their clients almost never express exactly what they want. The best way to overcome this obstacle is to show designers many examples of things that you like—advertisements from magazines, printouts from the Internet. If you like the color of your coffee mug, bring it with you to show your designer. Designers love to be in the position of having too many resources to design around as opposed to nothing.

Rest assured that you will be happier with the outcome if the designer can pick and choose elements of things you like rather than fish around in the dark. So now that you have provided the designer with bucketfuls of insight into what you like, does that ensure that you will like the results? Not necessarily, but we guarantee it will be closer to what you want.

The Nitty-Gritty

When hiring a designer, take the time to look at his or her portfolio, get recommendations from your colleagues, and ask for references.

Before you agree to work with a particular designer, make sure you know how many iterations of a design you will get and how many revisions you are allowed before extra charges apply. Typically there are three iterations and three revisions. For example, if you hired a designer to create a holiday card for you, you would be provided three to four different looks to choose from. Once you have narrowed down one look to proceed with, you then would be allowed three rounds of changes to the content and design before you started racking up additional charges.

Review Stage

This can be the make-it-or-break-it moment. The designer has taken all of your input and put it all together. You are either thrilled with the outcome or it just doesn't seem right.

If it doesn't seem right, then you need to articulate exactly what isn't working for you. That can be a hard thing to do, but rather than just say that it doesn't look right, try to be as specific as possible. Being specific doesn't mean that you tell the designer to move some text to the left an eighth of an inch.

These tips hopefully will help bridge the gap between you and your designer. You can't be afraid to say what you want, but you should also try to be open to the ideas and the feedback that the designer provides. Designers have a vested interest in making you look the best because their reputation is at stake.

Choosing a Designer

Choosing a designer can be a daunting task but a crucial one. If you aren't lucky enough to have an in-house designer, there are a quite a few options to help you find a freelance designer. A freelance designer is someone who will bid on design jobs as an individual practitioner rather than as a design firm or a full-time designer. In most cases, freelance designers are students looking to build their portfolios, designers who work as a full-time designer somewhere else and are looking to pick up some extra money or to round out their portfolio, or designers who make a living doing freelance work because they like the flexibility of picking and choosing which jobs they want to work on.

Working with a Design Firm versus a Freelancer

Design Firm
- You'll be guaranteed a higher-quality result (their reputation is on the line).
- You'll get help maintaining a consistent look throughout your different projects.
- Firms are generally more experienced working with vendors (can recommend cheaper alternatives).
- Firms can consult with you to make sure the execution you are pursuing will work for your target audience.
- Make sure to get references.
- Ask whether they have worked for a library or nonprofit before.
- They might be willing to do pro bono work if it can help raise their profile or aligns with their goals.
- You will have a built-in project manager (firms are deadline oriented; if they miss one, it throws off the other jobs).

Freelancer
- You'll typically pay much less.

- Freelancers are working to build a portfolio (so they will produce a high-quality result).
- Make sure to get references.
- Make sure to review their portfolio (if you are asking for print work, ask to see print work—don't go by web work).
- You can work with a different designer on each project to find out what visual style works for your target audience.
- Sometimes freelancers can offer faster turnaround times.
- You should have many more freelancers to choose from than design firms, so you can pick and choose who you want to work with.
- Cheaper prices typically result in lower-quality work.
- Freelancers can fly under the radar. If you are unhappy with their results, they can simply not provide you as a reference for future clients and no one would be the wiser (so take the time to find out as much about them as you can).

When searching for a freelancer or design firm, the best place to start is with your local chapter of the American Institute of Graphic Arts or the Art Directors Club. These groups, like any professional organization, have dues and guidelines for acceptable practices. If you choose a designer or firm from their directories, you ensure that the person or company has made an obligation to be professional and to follow those guidelines.

If you work at or around a university, you can usually solicit the design or arts department to see whether there are students available to do some freelance work for you. In addition, sites like www.craigslist.org, www.agaveblue.net, and www.guru.com are great places to find freelancers or to post your freelance jobs.

Usually, if you ask other institutions, departments, or nonprofits where you have contacts, they will be more than willing to make a recommendation for you. The same goes for any professional printers you may have worked with.

Finding Stock Photos, or... The Death of Clip Art

If you are on a tight budget or have someone on staff who wants to help, it might make sense for you to design your marketing materials in-house. A word of caution: there is nothing that screams amateur quite like clip art. Think about it. The public is bombarded with sophisticated graphics hundreds of times a day. If you create a disaster in Microsoft Publisher, chances are you are

Clip Art Alternatives

Library of Congress Prints and Photographs Collection (www .loc.gov). The Library of Congress provides free, super-high-resolution images from a selection of their catalog (growing every day); also a great place to browse for inspiration.

iStockphoto (www.istockphoto.com). This is a great, reasonably priced site with tons of illustrations, videos, and photography. You can either choose a subscription plan or pay as you go. If you pay as you go, you need to preload your account with credits that are sold in bundles of different sizes.

Shutterstock (www.shutterstock .com). This site is run on a subscription plan, and allows you to download seventy-five pictures a day for a reasonable flat rate.

Photos (www.photos.com). This is another subscription site.

FlickrStorm (www.zoo-m.com/ flickr-storm/). Here you can search Creative Commons–licensed photos from Flickr.

Veer (www.veer.com). This site is expensive but worth every penny. Impeccable quality, you can buy groups of stock images on CD that follow a specific theme or you can buy individual pictures.

doing more harm than good. If the packaging isn't nice, no one will bother to see what is inside.

It's easy to find free or really cheap high-quality images for your publications and marketing materials.

The quality of all of these pay sites vary. If you are downloading a ton of images in a month, then it makes sense for you to pay for a subscription plan (for a flat rate, you can download a certain number of images every day). If you are considering a subscription plan, take a week and evaluate the quality of each site's collection. Any time you think of an image that you would like to use, search each site and see which one has the closest image to what you envision. After doing this for a week or longer, subscribe to the site that garnered you the most results.

The free sites are typically a crapshoot, but they are always valuable for finding inspiration. If you are struggling to make your marketing message fit to a free image you found, it is time to break down and investigate the pay sites. If you are muddling your message so that it fits with the image, you are going to end up confusing customers. The image should reinforce the message, not the other way around.

Design Terminology

Here are a few terms that you should familiarize yourself with for working with printers or designers so that you can be aware of some of the aspects that affect the final product.

Dots per Inch (DPI)

Understanding dots per inch (sometimes called PPI, or pixels per inch) is crucial to working with print materials. A digital image's DPI (or resolution) is how many pixels are packed into every square inch of that image. When working with images that will be printed out, use images that have at least a 150 DPI. Anything less than that and your final printed image will start to look pixilated. Ideally, for printing you should use images that are 300 DPI. Images intended for the Web should all be 72 DPI.

A 72-dpi image (left) and a 300-dpi image (right) side by side.

You can easily convert any image to your desired DPI, but you will affect the final size of the image. For example, if you find an image on the Internet that is 8 inches wide and 10 inches tall at 72 DPI, when you convert it to 300 DPI the resulting image will only be 1.92 inches wide and 2.4 inches tall. The reverse is also true: if you take an 8-inch-by-10-inch image at 300 DPI, you'll have a 16-inch-by-20-inch image when you convert it to 150 DPI.

Quick notes:

Print—150 DPI or 300+ DPI (preferable)

Web—72 DPI

Vector Images

Vector images are resolution independent, which means that they can be increased in size indefinitely without losing quality. You will also hear vector images referred to as Illustrator files or EPS files. The scalability of vector images makes them perfect for things like logos and illustrations. If you are having a designer create a logo for you, make sure that you get a vector version of the logo so that you can use it on anything from the Web to a billboard without losing the image quality. (Vector illustrations can be photo-realistic; however, it greatly diminishes their ability to be scaled up.)

Our logo grabbed as a screen shot (top) from our website, and a vector version (bottom) with a detail blown up (inset).

Bleed

When a printer trims a stack of paper to size, the pressure of the blade coming down causes the paper to shift a little. To counteract this inconsistency, a designer will create a bleed by extending any color or image that flows off the edge of a printed piece. The amount of bleed is usually an eighth of an inch.

CMYK versus RGB

Both CMYK and RGB are formulas used to represent color in print or on the computer screen. Typically a color printer represents any color by printing differing amounts of cyan, magenta, yellow, and black onto a piece of paper. A computer monitor or a TV displays any color by varying amounts of red, green, and blue. So if a file will be used for print it should be created in or converted to CMYK color; if it is going to be used for the Web it should be created in or converted to RGB color.

Pantone

The Pantone Matching System (PMS) is a series of instructions on how to mix color for professional printers so that it is consistent, no matter what printer you use and what kind of stock it is used on. Usually you see Pantone colors specified in logos, so that the color(s) of your logo can be incorporated as part of your brand.

Professional Printers versus Ganged Printers versus Office Printers

Ganged Printers

Online print houses are usually ganged printers. Such printers usually offer incredibly low prices and limited paper choices. They can offer such low prices because they collect tons of jobs that will all be printed on the same paper (stock) and cut to the same size. Then they "gang" the jobs together by running them as one large job on the printer. This greatly reduces downtime and manpower. The trade-off for this quick and cheap process is a limited choice of paper and finished sizes as well as slightly degraded print quality.

Ganged printers:

www.jakprints.com

www.uprint.com

www.psprint.com

www.onlineprinthouse.com

Professional Printers

The price a printer quotes for a job can vary greatly from printer to printer depending on the specifications of that job. A printer that can do binding in-house will have a lower price than one that has to send it out to a bindery. Make sure that you get several quotes for your big print jobs. For the smaller ones, look into a ganged printer, or if you are trying to build a relationship with a professional printer that you have worked with in the past, it may be worth giving them the job if the price difference is fairly nominal. Once you build a relationship with a printer, they will start offering you discounts and offer to match other printers' quotes to maintain your business.

Increasingly, printer sales representatives have to know what is going on in the back of the house. They need to be knowledgeable about binding, paper stocks, and special processes like embossing or foil stamping. These sales reps can be invaluable to you; they can help you figure out a cheaper stock or how you can make your image really jump off the page.

Office Printers

Your office printer has a right place and a right time. Unless you have stock in a paper company, you will be limited to the paper you have on hand, and except for sort-of folding and double-sided printing, you won't have many finishing options. Even at Kinko's or the UPS Store, your options are pretty limited. Stick to the office printer when printing things for which quality isn't of utmost importance.

Printer Cheat Sheet

Ganged printer: Low cost, little choice, quick turnaround. Use for mailings or handouts for events, or when the turnaround time is more important than having options.

Professional printer: High cost, lots of options. Use when you need a professional look, such as for annual reports, donor-related event invitations, or when you need more options, such as for a multipage newsletter.

Office printer: Virtually no cost, no options. Use for marketing posters and bathroom newsletters.

A Note about Your Marketing and the Web

It is important to make sure that your marketing is represented on your website as well. It is easy to ignore your website and leave it to whomever maintains it. However, you need to become fast friends with the person maintaining the site. As your marketing evolves and grows, your website will increasingly need to reflect those changes. All of your marketing materials should point to the website as well. If you are having an event, have the registration online. If you are sending out a mailing, make the information available online and e-mail it to people who you can and physically mail it to the people you cannot reach digitally. Another great way to assess the effectiveness of your mailing is to put your website on the piece with a coded link. For example, if your website address is www.library.somewhere.edu, have your webmaster create a directory on the site that redirects the user to the home page—then the link you put on the mailed piece would be something like www.library.somewhere.edu/x (replace *x* with a keyword from the mailing). That way, when you are looking at your website statistics, you can see how many people accessed directory *x* as one way to access the mailing's effectiveness.

Branding

Branding is crucial to your marketing success; your marketing materials should be instantly recognizable the minute someone glances at them. The first step is to pick one or two fonts for use on every publication of the organization. The second step is to design or update your logo and make sure that it is used on anything and everything that the public might see. The third step is to become or appoint a brand czar.

Brand Czar

Every institution needs a brand czar who will make sure that every department or person who creates a publication associated with the library includes the basic elements of your library's brand.

To establish a brand czar, the first step is to create a style guide that lists the specific requirements and options for all library publications. The style guide should be easy to follow and have multiple options for correct usage. For example, if your official font is Verdana, you'll need to establish a backup font that is guaranteed to be found on all computers, such as Times New Roman. That way, the guide is flexible enough to be implemented.

A brand czar is someone at your institution who is the clearinghouse for any piece of information released to the public. This person makes sure that everyone adheres to the rules of the brand. They make sure that the text is set in the right font, that the logo is in the right place, that the color scheme matches the rest of the marketing, and, most important, that the quality is up to snuff.

A good procedure is to create a clearinghouse that reviews all external publications before production. This clearinghouse is your brand czar. Depending on the size of your institution, it might be wise to establish a formal procedure. The policies and style guides would be distributed broadly and easily accessible. A training program would be developed to educate staff about the importance of the cohesive brand, with tangible examples of good and bad practices. Each department would update its standard operating procedures to reflect the brand czar as the clearinghouse.

Essential action step: create the style guide. The brand czar is important, but your first step must be to set the standards for your brand. Don't worry if you're not happy with your logo; instead worry about creating visual consistency now to lay the groundwork for that new logo when you get it.

Some people will say that this will squelch their creativity. Others may see it is making the library boring, too standardized, too corporate. They might be right, and we just need to remind ourselves that brand consistency is paramount in this age of cluttered information overload.

What do we do with the people who have fallen in love with Microsoft Publisher and enjoy making their own stuff? Why not use their talent on internal marketing, like staff newsletters? But it's probably just better to keep educating and hope they'll come into the fold.

What about those times when you want to break out of the brand? No exceptions. Remember the big picture and why you're doing it.

If we establish ourselves as players in the community by using our brand, we'll have a lot more flexibility to be creative with our programs, products, and services.

Baby Steps to Branding

1. Choose two fonts (one serif and one sans-serif) that you can use in all publications in a combination of the three or by themselves.
2. Pick three colors and use them exclusively in all publications.
3. Use your logo on every publication.
4. Create a shared area where you can display all of your existing publications—invite staff to see the different styles used. They will most surely see why branding is essential after that.
5. Communicate to staff the role of branding in the current environment.

Elements of a Brand

☐ Logo
☐ Color palette
☐ Fonts
☐ Style guide

Branded Materials

☐ Stationery
☐ Business cards
☐ Web
☐ Brochures
☐ Newsletter
☐ Posters

☐ Advertisements
☐ Bookmarks
☐ Fax cover sheet
☐ E-mail
☐ Building signage

Marketing Best Practices

10

Repositioning

Repositioning allows us to change the identity of the library and put it in stark contrast to the competition. Start a conversation in your organization with the following questions:

1. What is the traditional role of the library?
2. How has this role changed since the advent of the Internet?
3. What do we do better than our competition?
4. What do we do that is different from our competition?
5. How do we want our target market to see us as compared to the competition?

The answer to these questions will help you to reposition your identity.

Getting to Know Your Audience

Let's say you have decided that you would like to increase teen participation in after-school programs at the library. What are teens thinking about? Who do they look up to? What kind of music do they like? Movies? What else? This is the time for you to do some market research! Market research is any research that you do to understand the buying habits of a particular audience.

Think of every ad you see or hear as research material.

Important Things to Look For

What does your age group wear?

What does your age group read?

Magazines

Books

Websites, blogs, and the like

What does your age group talk about with one another?

What kinds of music does your age group listen to?

Observe the group members in their natural habitat—in this case, the mall. If you can look at and listen to this group without your own biases, you will create a teen program that will really appeal to them.

Also look at how others market to your age group—as you can imagine, for-profit marketing always has a bigger budget than nonprofit marketing like libraries, so take the time to analyze the marketing targeted to the age group you are interested in.

- What color palettes are used? Hey, those companies just spent millions of dollars figuring that out. Take advantage so you don't have to spend that money.
- Who are the influencers or spokespeople (Miley Cyrus or major sports figures)?
- What is the language being used? This is a very slippery one. There is nothing worse than a person who is outside a particular age group using slang inappropriately, so do so sparingly.

Be Aware of Marketing and Design Everywhere

- Don't just watch TV; analyze it. What ads play at what time? What ads appeal to what values? What colors, spokespeople, and themes are dominant?
- Look at magazines. If you are a woman, look at men's health magazines. If you are a man, look at women's fashion magazines. Look at magazines for teens, for tweens, for young adults, and so on. In these, what colors, spokespeople, and themes are dominant?
- When you are in stores, ask yourself the same questions about colors, spokespeople, and themes.

Assessment

One of the easiest ways to get honest opinions about your library is to run some focus groups. Often you can entice certain populations to engage in a focus group by buying them lunch—this works well with students. Another way to encourage people to attend focus groups is to give each member a gift card from locally owned businesses. This helps the library build relationships with the community by assuring local businesses that you support the local community and not a faceless global chain.

Advisory Group

If you think running a focus group is complicated, you can instead start with an advisory committee. This is an informal group brought together to tell you the truth from their personal point of view. You can start by asking a club that already exists, such as student government, the parent-teacher association, or service clubs.

Some caveats to keep in mind:

- You have to be ready to hear negative things.
- Some things people ask for will be too expensive.
- You have to learn to listen to users with a nonjudgmental ear.
- This is a one-way conversation, one of those rare occasions where you are not there to talk them into loving the library.
- You should only ask questions, not talk at the group.

Usability Testing

You can also engage in usability testing, which is when you ask patrons very specific questions about finding things on your website and observe the path that they take to get there.

The similarity between all these different forms of feedback is that you must listen without inserting your opinion or leading the conversation in any way. You want the patrons to tell you exactly what they think about your resources, services, or whatever you are asking them about.

Sometimes this information is hard to hear and even harder to understand. So it is very important to find someone who can ask the questions impartially without becoming emotionally invested in the answers. Also, you must ask a lot of clarification questions without leading.

You can also use groups that already exist, such as a teen group, a book group, or another regularly meeting group. You probably want to ask them no more than three questions. On a college campus, you might work with the student government or a student group.

Although it is very difficult to do so, you should try to find ways to reach nonusers of the library, because you want to try to find out what the obstacles are that these groups face and how to remove them.

Assessment can come in many different forms. Creating a culture of assessment requires the organization to always think about what it wants to measure. For example:

- Number of attendees at programs such as storytimes, classes, workshops, musical events, or lectures
- Number of resources used: books checked out, database searches, or digital collection views

Corporate Sponsorship

Getting corporate sponsorship for your library events is easy if you follow a few simple steps.

1. Define the type of sponsor you want to go after: you always want to make sure that a business knows that you picked it for a specific reason. For example, you might call a sporting-goods store to sponsor a video game night at the library. You explain to the store that you chose it because your target audience is teenage boys ages twelve to seventeen. Obviously, this age group frequents sporting-goods stores and wears sports attire. You can tell the store that it seems great for them to sponsor a library event and that you would like to provide your target audience with some gifts.

2. Write up a sample sponsor letter. Each store or organization that sponsors you usually needs to show or have proof that they are giving away goods to someone legitimate. In the letter, write a one-line description of the event, the rationale for having the event, and one goal of the event. Always make sure to tell the sponsor how many attendees you expect. Then tailor each letter to the sponsor.

3. Be tenacious. Sometimes you have to call your contact several times to secure sponsorship. Remember that these people are as busy as you are, so until they say no, continue to call and write. Keep track of each time you make contact so that you do not call them too little or too much.

4. Ask the sponsor for a camera-ready logo to put on your posters. Explain to sponsors when and how you will use their logos and how many people will be exposed to the logo. Once again, this is great for the sponsor's public image, so it is a win-win situation.

5. Follow up with thank-you cards and details of how the event went. If you want to continue building a list of all possible sponsors for different events, make sure to follow up and thank them.

To-Dos:

1. Define the type of sponsor you want.

2. Write up a sample sponsor letter.

3. Be tenacious.

4. Ask the sponsor for a print-ready logo.

5. Follow up with a thank-you card.

It seems to me that you can do the survey thing, the focus group thing, the visioning thing, etc., and we have done all of the above, but the most effective thing is the involvement of all staff in the community. Here, in Charlotte, all staff members have a responsibility for publicity for their programs, all provide programs and all spend as much time as possible becoming involved in the community. For example, I am involved in two service clubs, am vice-chairman of the city planning commission, I attend township meetings, am out speaking to groups, talking with the public as often as the opportunity presents itself. Each staff member, and there are 19 of us, does the same. At our monthly staff meetings, we all bring our ideas, concerns and problems to the fore. No idea or comment is looked down upon. If something comes to the fore and needs to be brought out more than once a month, staff brings the information or problem to me directly. We also have an ongoing, online journal, read and contributed to by all staff.

—William Siarny, *library director, Charlotte Community Library, Michigan*

Internal Marketing

Marketing is relatively new to libraries. Before the widespread use of the Internet, people who wanted to research a specific topic had limited choices. Two of the most used sources were to go to a bookstore and buy a book, magazine, or newspaper or to go to the library and borrow a book and/or copy a magazine or newspaper. Obviously, the choices for finding information have multiplied and exploded in the past fifteen years, and libraries no longer have a monopoly on information. In other words, we are no longer the gatekeepers of information. In marketing terms, we need to reposition our brand. We need to find ways to raise awareness of our vital role in our communities and articulate the role that libraries play in the new information landscape.

But before we create external marketing for our libraries, we have to get the internal organization comfortable with marketing. We have to introduce people to many different concepts of marketing, such as branding,

Internal marketing is all of the communication that you have with the members of your organization throughout the life of your marketing campaign.

visual consistency, communication vehicles, and channels. Most of these marketing concepts may be new to employees who have worked in educational organizations or nonprofits for most of their careers. Internal marketing is the communication you have with the members of your organization about marketing and their role in it.

Are You Ready to Market?

Use this quick form to assess your organization's level of need for internal marketing.

Do employees know the shared values, mission, and goals (VMGs) that the organization embraces? ☐ YES ☐ NO	**If no**, review them (if they need to be updated, now is the time to revise). **If yes**, show how your marketing goals can align to your VMGs. This is a basic check and balance that marketers often use. First, go over each VMG and explain how your marketing efforts will help the organization live up to them. If you cannot make the connection, then you'll need to revaluate your marketing goals.	**Outcome**: The people in your organization will understand the role of marketing in supporting the VMGs.
Does your organization feel as though no one knows what he or she is doing? ☐ YES ☐ NO	**If no**, fantastic, you are an extraordinary marketer and deserve a raise. **If yes**, it's time to start talking about the M word. Most libraries are just now becoming comfortable with marketing, and this is the perfect time to embrace it.	**Outcome**: The people in your organization will begin to understand the role of marketing in articulating your value.

Do the people in your organization wish your library's promotional materials had a more cohesive look? ☐ YES ☐ NO	**If no**, then it's time to create a publication wall. **If yes**, then its time to create a style sheet.	**Outcome**: The people in your organization will begin to see the value in creating a consistent look.
When you launch your marketing plan, do you have the staff and resources to back up what you are promising? ☐ YES ☐ NO	**If no**, it's time to evaluate your marketing goals or make a contingency plan to reallocate your resources. **If yes**, then you are ready to roll out your marketing campaign.	**Outcome**: The people in your organization will have confidence and are able to deliver the marketing goals you've set.

Demystifying Marketing for Staff

Another aspect that is important in internal marketing is demystifying marketing in general for libraries. Most people who come to work in a library see themselves as outside the corporate world. Marketing traditionally has been thought of as deceitful or overly corporate, but in actuality it is about communicating your values to your customers. Marketing for libraries is a powerful way for libraries to accomplish our goals and stay relevant. In her phenomenal book *Robin Hood Marketing: How to Steal Corporate Savvy to Sell Just Causes*, Katya Andersen says: "There is no nobility in preaching to an audience of one. Those of us working for the public good have an ethical responsibility to be effective and efficient in reaching as many people as possible."

Marketing is about communicating values clearly and concisely.

As Andersen points out so eloquently, we have to see marketing as an ethical responsibility. If we know that the services and resources that we provide for people make their lives better, we can step away from our commercialized view of marketing and move on to creating marketing programs that we can be proud of and fully invest ourselves in.

Internal Marketing Ideas

Create a Publication Wall

1. Gather all of your current publications.
2. Put them all up in a place where they can be viewed together.
3. Are there many different looks and treatments in the publications?
4. Are there different colors, fonts, and designs used in publications?
5. Are there too many publications going out? Could some of the publications be combined?
6. Does this exercise make it clear that library publications need a more consistent look?

Hold an Open House

Once you are far enough along in your campaign—after you and your team have created key messages and are beginning to think about the look and design—create mock-ups and hold an open house to see what library staff think about your direction.

Find different ways for staff to provide feedback during open houses. Some examples include the following:

- Note cards for employees' comments.
- Members of the marketing committee talking with and recording feedback from staff.
- A sign-up sheet for departments, teams, or committees to use if they want the marketing team to come to their meetings.
- A follow-up time for staff to come and speak to the marketing committee.

Keep Employees Informed

Update employees through appropriate communication channels available in your organization. Remember that updating does not mean boring people with too much detail.

- Use staff meetings to update employees and ask for feedback.
- Talk informally and individually with employees.
- Send out executive summaries of the marketing committee's work via e-mail.
- Create a marketing portfolio with all of the designs you have created with the corresponding style sheet—you can do this in hard copy or invite people to electronically view the information and comment.

Take the time to document your marketing best practices so that you can build the institutional knowledge of your marketing campaigns.

Succession Planning

Succession planning is very important in marketing, as it enables you to build institutional knowledge and create a foundation for future projects. Even more important, succession planning enables you to hand off projects to people who want to replicate best practices. Finally, a succession plan will allow people other than founding members of the marketing committee to continue projects. We are all pressed for time and this is the easiest way to not reinvent the wheel

Ways to Start Succession Planning

- Make a master calendar—input events, programs, deadlines for publications, and so on.

- Create and maintain a list of community and campus contacts.

- Create and maintain a list of volunteers who have helped with past events.

- Create and maintain a list of equipment.

- Create and maintain a list of media contacts.

- Create and maintain a list of corporate sponsors and what they have given you.

- Save copies of press releases.

- Compile copies of designs.

- Compile information about all presentations made about marketing.

- Compile all budget documentation.

- Save copies of time lines.

Use all of this material to create a portfolio that can be used to educate new staff about previous marketing initiatives.

Index